What people are saying about ...

Straight to the Heart

"*Straight to the Heart* is a timely, insightful, and impactful book. Mike and Daniel rightly recognize that we need to adapt our evangelistic and apologetic strategies to meet the state of our culture. And yet, I deeply appreciate that, while they recognize we live in an emotionally driven culture, this does not mean we abandon the mind. Communicating the gospel today means rightly engaging both. I highly recommend this book."

Sean McDowell, PhD, professor of apologetics
at Biola University and author or co-author
of over 20 books including *Set Adrift*

"*Straight to the Heart* is essential reading for anyone who wants to understand the times. But more than that, this book is a rich, beautiful exploration of what it means to be human in a more holistic way. *Straight to the Heart* will serve all believers, not only in reaching other people with the gospel, but simply in helping us to live more fully and completely as creatures of head and heart, as God designed us to be."

Karen Swallow Prior, author of *The Evangelical Imagination*

"A refreshingly holistic account of how we address both the head and the heart in today's frantic culture. Those frustrated by a generation of younger people who seem to be led by nothing more than their emotions will find this book to be both encouraging and challenging in equal measure."

Kenneth Boa, founder, Reflections
Ministries, Museum of Created Beauty

"This transformative book is an invitation to trade your fears and frustrations for hope and excitement as you are inspired to introduce a disheartened culture to fulfillment in Christ. With profound, real-life insight into the intersection of gospel and culture, Mike and Daniel Blackaby refuse our cultural ultimatum of truth or love, instead illuminating the beauty found in a holistic apologetic committed to loving the whole person. As deeply perceptive as it is highly readable, *Straight to the Heart* is like sitting down with one of the most stimulating people you know in the place where you feel most at home."

Vince Vitale, PhD, author of *Non-Identity Theodicy*

"Brothers Mike and Daniel extend to us an exciting and compelling invitation to join them in engaging the hearts of future generations. *Straight to the Heart* is a concise primer for accessing their potential by appealing to their hearts through the ancient art of storytelling. Students in our schools and ministers in our churches need to read this book carefully and then make immediate application of the realities revealed there."

Rob Blackaby, PhD, president of Canadian
Baptist Theological Seminary & College

"The emphasis on emotions in our culture presents a challenge for presenting gospel truth. Rather than lamenting cultural change, the Blackaby brothers have written a grammar for believers to converse in the 'heart language' of emotion, which, it turns out, is a native tongue of Scripture. *Straight to the Heart* helps Christians to tell the beautiful story of the gospel in a way that stirs the desires of those who hear it and invites them to enter the story as those who have received the grace of King Jesus."

Cory Barnes, PhD, dean of Doctoral Studies and Distance Learning, New Orleans Baptist Theological Seminary

"*Straight to the Heart* is a must read for any believer who has a desire to reach and affect the heart of culture with the beauty and truth of God. Mike and Daniel not only take the great commission very seriously but have put deep thought and study into how best to live that out. With confidence and clarity, they give us a practical and inspiring vision for how to speak the language of those around us, particularly the ones we don't see eye to eye with, always with the goal of introducing a loving and redemptive God to a world desperately in need. This book is a necessity for any artist, teacher, or preacher."

Nathan Clarkson, *Publishers Weekly*-bestselling author, award-winning TV and film actor, indie filmmaker

"*Straight to the Heart* compellingly describes why the declining evangelism effectiveness of the Western Church is more the fruit of an unconvinced and unconvincing mission force than it is of an unprepared and uninterested mission field. Through insightful biblical and cultural exegeses, Mike and Daniel Blackaby diagnose our spiritual malady and then prescribe a spiritual balm. The answers provided are not complicated—but they are costly. Highly recommend."

Jeff Christopherson, executive director of the Canadian National Baptist Convention, and author of *Once You See*

"History is marked by hard pivots—economically, linguistically, theologically, and intellectually. *Straight to the Heart* identifies the recent intellectual pivot in the West that prioritizes heart over head, emotions over logic. Its analysis outlines a gospel-centered approach to navigating the pivot as Christians seek to share their faith with their neighbors. Simultaneously erudite and readable, the approach holds great promise, especially for those steeped in the older way of communicating Truth but desirous of helping others approach it faithfully and transformationally."

Gene C. Fant, Jr., professor of English and president, North Greenville University, and author of *God as Author*

MIKE BLACKABY & DANIEL BLACKABY

STRAIGHT TO THE
HEART

COMMUNICATING THE GOSPEL IN
AN EMOTIONALLY DRIVEN CULTURE

DAVID C COOK

transforming lives together

STRAIGHT TO THE HEART
Published by David C Cook
4050 Lee Vance Drive
Colorado Springs, CO 80918 U.S.A.

Integrity Music Limited, a Division of David C Cook
Brighton, East Sussex BN1 2RE, England

DAVID C COOK® and related marks are registered trademarks of David C Cook.

The website addresses recommended throughout this book are offered as a
resource to you. These websites are not intended in any way to be or imply an
endorsement on the part of David C Cook, nor do we vouch for their content.

Library of Congress Control Number: 2023945308
ISBN 978-0-8307-8584-1
eISBN 978-0-8307-8585-8

The Team: Luke McKinnon, Stephanie Bennett, Jeff Gerke, Gina
Pottenger, Leigh Davidson, James Hershberger, Susan Murdock
Interior illustrations on pages 48 and 135
courtesy of Sarah Emily Blackaby
Cover Design: Joe Cavazos

Printed in the United States of America
First Edition 2024

1 2 3 4 5 6 7 8 9 10

032324

We dedicate this book to our grandmother,
Marilynn Blackaby. She often turned complete
strangers into lifelong friends by her ability to
speak the "heart language." Culture ebbs and
flows but loving people never goes out of style. She
loved well and, in turn, was greatly loved.

Contents

Introduction

Kids These Days

Not long ago, I (Daniel) was invited to speak at a Christian conference in Tennessee. I was the (relatively) young guy on the program tasked with challenging the audience to engage the culture and reach the younger generation.

Before the session, as I stood alone near the stage reviewing my notes, a middle-aged man approached me with a stack of books in his hands. The titles were familiar to me as popular works of apologetics. In the morning session, the emcee mentioned I had done doctoral studies in the area of Christian apologetics, so this man wanted to hear my opinions on the books.

As we talked, I quickly discerned two things about him. The first was that he clearly had a passion for passing on his faith to the younger generations, both as a father and as a dedicated layperson in his church. The second was a sense of hopelessness bordering on frustration—even anger—about how to do so.

"Kids these days just don't have any firm foundation in truth," he declared, growing increasingly animated. "They're all driven by their emotions and feelings." He listed off several examples, from the "snowflakes" on college campuses to the "woke" ideologies perpetuated through Hollywood. "We need to ground them in the *truth*," he continued, shaking one of the apologetics books. I wasn't sure if he meant to use the rational arguments contained inside or to use the hardback book to beat the emotions out of these wayward prodigals!

The longer we spoke, the more evident it became that his passion was coming from a good place. His concern was inspired by several young adults he had personally invested in who had later drifted away from church, swept up in the ideologies and trends of the world. He lamented the path they had chosen and was committed to equipping himself with enough rational arguments to counterbalance the culture's spiral into the emotional, experiential, and aesthetic.

Our conversation was cut short as music played to begin the session. I found my seat and frantically reevaluated my notes, which no longer seemed as profound or insightful as they had that morning. I had come with the best answers I could muster on the topic, but now I had experienced the question embodied in the flesh. The lecture was no longer abstract. It was personal.

The audience was polite and responsive, but I'm not sure if my presentation had as much impact as I'd hoped. Perhaps the more important talk that evening was that presession conversation. My lecture was likely forgotten by the crowd, but my encounter with that man lingered in my mind long after the conference was over.

Has the World Lost Its Mind?

Since that day, we have encountered this concern many times and in various forms. A growing number of Christians are uneasy about the direction the world (and the church) seems to be heading. It looks like the world has lost its mind, and many Christians find themselves wondering how to navigate this new landscape.

Of course, *every* generation looks at their culture and asks, "What is going on?" Parents shake their heads at the fashion choices of their children, and the bewilderment is often reciprocated when their kids stumble across photos of their parents from "back in the day." But it goes deeper than the latest goofy hairstyle or tightness of jeans. Often what is unthinkable in one generation is flirted with by the following one and fully embraced by the next.

This has always been true of ideas and trends, but there seems to be something distinctive about the present cultural situation. David Kinnaman, president of the research organization Barna Group, has referred to this culture as "discontinuously different."[1]

Much of the anxiety within the church about the state of the culture is due to a perceived paradigm shift regarding not just *what* society thinks but also *how* it thinks. The emerging generations appear to have minimized the head (logic, reason, evidence) in order to elevate the heart (emotions, intuitions, aesthetics). Heightened passions are the order of the day. Conversations built on basic shared assumptions are becoming rare as each individual seeks "*my* truth" rather than *the* truth. Whether it's political arguments on social media, activists on college campuses, or the changing tides of social opinions on sexuality and gender, it can be a bewildering landscape to traverse.

Changing Terrain

Difficult as it may be, Christians *must* navigate this new terrain, and our ability or inability to do so will have far-reaching consequences. Though the church has become more proficient at articulating the truth of Scripture through sound apologetic answers to difficult rational objections, we appear to be losing our cultural footprint at an alarming rate. More and more, those outside the church are not just disinterested in Christianity but also disillusioned and even repelled by it.

Christians are called to be "salt" that prevents rot in our culture and "light" that shines brightly in the darkness (Matt. 5:13–16). We are to be distinctly different *from* the world but also an active presence *within* it (John 17:14–19). We are commissioned into the mission of making disciples of all nations (Matt. 28:16–20; Acts 1:8). Because of this calling, we must do more than "get by" in a world gone mad. We need to approach what lies ahead effectively for the kingdom of God.

The same trends that are happening "out there" are increasingly evident within the church as well. Many young adults are growing apathetic toward the faith of their youth, driven to deconstruct their negative religious experiences, and more drawn to the picture of life offered by a secular culture than the one presented in the church. Alarmingly, many of these young adults have been exposed to biblical teaching for years, yet they continue to jump ship as soon as their independence allows them the opportunity. In fact, often their decision is not in spite of the church's teachings but because of them.

> If we want to communicate effectively
> to a Heart Culture, we must learn to
> converse in the language of the heart.

Christians are called to communicate an unchanging faith in a rapidly changing world. Yet there is an emerging disconnect between the message we are proclaiming and how it is being received both by those who are outside the church and those inside who are eyeing the exits. The cultural paradigm has changed—a "Head Culture," if you will, has morphed into a "Heart Culture"—and many Christians find themselves at a loss for how to speak in the new scenario.

Here We Are ... Now What?

"How did we get here?" Much ink and video bandwidth has been dedicated to answering that question. We will examine certain important chapters of that story, but the truth is that countless factors have contributed to the rise of the current Heart Culture. In whatever way the Cave of Wonders was found, and however Aladdin's lamp got rubbed, the proverbial genie cannot easily be put back inside. The burning question is, "Now what?"

In J. R. R. Tolkien's *The Lord of the Rings,* when Frodo, a humble hobbit from the peaceful Shire, laments over the evil state of the world, he receives timely counsel from the wise wizard Gandalf:

> It is not our part to master all the tides of the world,
> but to do what is in us for the succour of those years
> wherein we are set, uprooting the evil in the fields
> that we know, so that those who live after may have
> clean earth to till. What weather they shall have is
> not ours to rule.[2]

As the church, we should not spend our time wishing the situation were different. Our task is to live faithfully in the years allotted to us and to ask God how we shall live "for such a time as this" (Est. 4:14b).

Theologian and historian Carl Trueman puts it more bluntly: "The task of the Christian is not to whine about the moment in which he or she lives but to understand its problems and respond appropriately to them."[3]

Our primary concern in this book is not to focus on how things got to this point.* Rather, since this is the time in which God has placed us, we must ask how we should best respond to the unique challenges of our day.

Challenges and Opportunities

A central Scripture for how Christians are to approach an unbelieving culture is 1 Peter 3:15: "But in your hearts revere Christ as Lord. Always be prepared to give an answer to everyone who asks you to give the reason for the hope that you have. But do this with gentleness and respect."† When the unbelieving world questions, resists, or rejects our spiritual convictions, Christians begin with our internal faith ("your hearts"), and then translate and articulate that reality externally for the person asking the questions ("give an answer").

Like the man in the opening of this introduction, many well-meaning Christians want to meet this challenge. They are prepared to rationally converse with the culture, but they seem to have hit a dead end with no way forward. After all, how can you have a rational discussion with someone who seems unwilling to be rational?

---

* For a good historical and philosophical account of how culture got to this place, refer to Carl Trueman's *The Rise and Triumph of the Modern Self*, or his shorter version, *Strange New World: How Thinkers and Activists Redefined Identity and Sparked the Sexual Revolution* (Wheaton, IL: Crossway, 2022).

† The Greek word translated as "give an answer" is *apologia*, which is where the term "apologetics" comes from.

A dead end is truly a stopping point only if there's no other path forward. In 1 Peter 3:15, there are two elements at play: a question and a response. Could it be that we have become accustomed to beginning with the answer and have grown frustrated that the world is no longer asking the "right" questions? What if we started with a posture of listening and then shaped our response to most effectively communicate the hope of Jesus to the questions our culture is actually asking? What opportunities might arise out of these changing cultural trends?

In Gary Chapman's classic book on relationships, *The Five Love Languages*, he notes that everyone desires to be loved, but we communicate and receive love in different "languages."[4] One individual may genuinely try to express love to another, but if that person is not speaking the "language" that is most natural to the *other* person, it can lead to frustration rather than intimacy. A husband may try to love his wife using the language that makes the most sense to him, such as "words of affirmation," but if her love language is "physical touch," then one hug will speak louder to her than a hundred kind words.

Might it be that our culture longs to know the love of God expressed through His gospel, but we have not learned to speak in the language they best understand? If we want to communicate effectively to a Heart Culture, we must learn to converse in the language of the heart.

Straight to the Heart

When navigating a culture that has lost its head, so to speak, we need not follow them to the guillotine! The answer for how to respond to an irrational culture is not to forsake the rational foundation of biblical truth. In fact, the way forward is not to subtract something, but to add—or perhaps, remember—an important truth: God speaks to our hearts. He always has.

To effectively connect with a world driven by its affections, Christians must first rediscover that we are *all* emotional beings created in the image of a God who is both Clockmaker and Divine Artist. A God whose revelation of Himself is found in the Bible, where theological teaching (e.g., Romans, Hebrews) exists alongside captivating narrative (e.g., the Gospels, 1 and 2 Samuel); a collection of books that includes the poetic heights of ecstasy (e.g., Song of Songs, Psalms) as well as the depths of doom and despair (e.g., Lamentations, the Prophets).

When God initiates contact with us, it is always directed to both head and heart, intellect and emotion, propositional facts and experiential truths.

For a time, while operating within a primarily rational Head Culture, it was appropriate and effective to engage on more analytical terms. Now, though, emotion is granted the highest authority. We are operating within a Heart Culture, both inside and outside the church. As we put our finger on the pulse to discover the affections that drive people, we will not only elevate our encounters with the culture, we will also come to understand our own faith in a fresh way.

Perhaps you can relate to the man at the beginning of this chapter. You are driven by a genuine desire to share God's love and truth with the culture around you but feel like you are not getting through. An emotionally and aesthetically driven culture may seem like less fertile soil for rational discourse, but rationality is not the only language available to us.

Instead of growing frustrated with a culture that places such high value on emotion, aesthetics, and narrative, let's explore what it looks like to meet them in that place. In a culture driven by affections, we can draw close to a God who satisfies those deepest desires, and then communicate His truth straight to their hearts.

Part 1

Learning the
Heart Language

Chapter 1

A Culture That Lost Its Mind (but Found Its Heart)

"But I don't want to go among mad people," said Alice.
"Oh, you can't help that," said the Cat: "we're all mad here."
—Lewis Carroll, *Alice's Adventures in Wonderland*

The heart has its reasons of which reason
knows nothing: we know this in countless ways.
—Blaise Pascal

A Mad World

Mark Twain famously quipped that "truth is stranger than fiction."[1] He made a good point. Turning on the news or scrolling through social media may cause you to feel like Alice in Lewis Carroll's *Alice's Adventures in Wonderland*, having fallen down the rabbit hole and emerged into a land that feels upside down. In this strange new world, people seem to echo the Queen of Wonderland in declaring, "Sometimes I've believed as many as six impossible things before breakfast."[2] Much of the societal bedrock (not to mention common-sense observation) that once seemed immovable in our culture has been challenged, redefined, or discarded.

From a faith perspective, Christians don't face new objections to their beliefs as much as a new paradigm. For years, modernity was the familiar backdrop for cultural engagement, with standard debates such as Darwinism versus creationism or miracles versus science. A postmodern culture has not only updated the game board with new pieces, it has entirely rewritten the rules. Christians do not face a barrage of new rational arguments but an abandonment of reason itself (or so it seems).

The Christ-given mission to go into the world and make disciples (Matt. 28:16–20) is not contingent on a preferable cultural paradigm. The call is to *go*, whatever lies ahead. Thus, we must scout a path forward. To do so, we can be guided by three important questions:

1. How did we get here?
2. What is the new Heart Culture paradigm?
3. How can the church respond?

Let's begin with a story.

Country of the Blind

In *The Country of the Blind*, a short book by science fiction pioneer H. G. Wells, a mountaineer named Nunez falls down a slope into a deep valley and discovers the fabled Country of the Blind. Many years earlier, an earthquake had shifted the geography and isolated the once-prosperous village. Then a mysterious illness had spread, causing all babies to be born blind.

Nunez attempts to explain vision to the country's sightless inhabitants, but they mock his ramblings and deem his obsession with sight madness. The blind dwellers of the valley have adapted to their condition and now navigate their surroundings using other means. As a seeing man in a society built by the blind, Nunez is clumsy and awkward to them, like a child learning to walk.

From H.G. Wells's story *The Country of the Blind,* published in *The Strand Magazine* in April 1904

Wikimedia Commons: Illustration by Claude Allin Shepperson

In order to adapt to the situation, Nunez eventually relents and settles into living as a functionally sightless man. He soon falls in love, but when he asks for the young lady's hand in marriage, the village elders refuse due to his fixation on sight. They decide that the only solution is to surgically remove his eyes, putting an end to his apparent delusions. Out of love, he reluctantly agrees.

As the day of the surgery approaches, Nunez feels the magnitude of his impending sacrifice. He realizes that he will never again see the sublime beauty in the world or the good things beyond the mountains. As he gazes at their peaks, he suddenly spots a crack in the mountain. It had been growing over time, but in his self-imposed blindness, he had not recognized it. Then he sees another fissure develop, shifting the massive stones. The mountain is about to fall, and the rockslide will surely destroy the village. Nunez quickly descends back into the valley to warn the villagers. Although most dismiss the warning as the rambling of a madman, Nunez and his betrothed manage to flee just as the slide crashes into the village.

To engage with the blind, Nunez set aside his vision to find common ground. In a land where all the wonders that eyes can see seemed irrelevant, his vision was an obstacle to connecting with the villagers. In the process, he became comfortable with his self-imposed limitations, and "the world beyond the mountains became more and more remote and unreal."[3] But a new challenge presented itself that required him to embrace his neglected sense of sight, or else risk being annihilated by the landslide.

The church today is in a similar position. We can identify with Nunez in *The Country of the Blind* because our own narrative began with the church choosing to accommodate the most immediate challenge of modernity: meeting the Head Culture with rational arguments for truth. However, like Nunez, the church risked losing sight of the bigger picture as the rockslide of Heart Culture tumbled into the valley.

Question 1: How Did We Get Here?
Previous Rules of Engagement

In the 2000s, a movement called New Atheism rose to prominence. Their spokespersons took an antagonistic posture toward religion. They were evidently disappointed that the famous 1966 *Time* magazine cover asking "Is God Dead?" failed to answer the question with a definitive "yes," especially in America where belief in God remains high.*

---

* While trending downward, 81% of Americans still answered "yes" when a recent Gallup poll asked the simple question, "Do you believe in God?" Lydia Saad and Zach Hrynowski, "How Many Americans Believe in God?," Gallup, June 24, 2022, https://news.gallup.com/Poll/268205/Americans-Believe-God.Aspx.

The New Atheists argued that religious belief was blind faith in the face of contrary rational evidence. They portrayed believers as uncritical, unthinking, and irrational (to put it mildly ... which they often didn't). Atheist Sam Harris wrote:

> Whatever their imagined source, the doctrines of modern religions are no more tenable than those which, for lack of adherents, were cast upon the scrap heap of mythology millennia ago; for there is no more evidence to justify a belief in the literal existence of Yahweh and Satan than there was to keep Zeus perched upon his mountain throne or Poseidon churning the seas.[4]

In a rational Head Culture, religion failed the entrance exam: "It is time that we admitted that faith is nothing more than the license religious people give one another to keep believing when reasons fail."[5] New Atheists' books topped bestseller charts and gained a quick following, often composed of others who were angry at religion.

A Rational Response

In response to New Atheism, many intelligent Christians rose to the occasion and defended the rationality of faith.[†] They published books, wrote articles, and engaged in public debates. This led to a revival in the study of apologetics in churches and Bible schools. Suddenly, an

---

[†] Such as William Lane Craig, Richard Swinburne, Gary Habermas, Nancy Pearcey, Lee Strobel, Alvin Plantinga, J. P. Moreland, Alister McGrath, Timothy Keller, Paul Copan, John Lennox, Frank Turek, Mary Jo Sharp, Sean McDowell, and Gregory Koukl, among others.

army of church youth group kids were being equipped to converse with their unbelieving classmates using ontological and cosmological arguments for God's existence.†

Browsing the titles of the books written during this time reveals a clear theme: *Reasonable Faith, Faith Has Its Reasons, The Reason for God, Faith and Rationality*, etc. Within this climate, the movie *God's Not Dead* (2014) grossed an impressive $62 million. The film's premise exemplified the church's mindset toward the Head Culture: universities are filled with atheist professors eager to pluck young people out of the church, and the only response is to equip our students with rational arguments to defend themselves.

The church wisely engaged their opposition on the playing field of the other's choosing, which was the realm of reason, science, logic, and empirical evidence. Like Nunez in *The Country of the Blind*, Christians responded to the villagers in a way that fit the current situation, and it sparked an important resurgence in critical thinking within the church. Yet, while we were engaging the New Atheists, a rockslide was developing on the other side of the ravine ...

Incoming!

There's a trope in Hollywood that whenever two titanic forces are pitted against each other, inevitably a third player will emerge that threatens to overpower both (see *Godzilla vs. Kong* or *Batman v Superman: Dawn of Justice*).

---

† We were two of those young adults and are grateful for many of these books and videos that shaped our worldview. Both of us ultimately did doctoral work in the field of apologetics. Mike wrote his dissertation as a critique of Sam Harris's worldview.

As Christian apologists and the New Atheists battled it out in the boxing ring of rationality, something else manifested: society became a culture of the heart. Many of the fundamental aspects of the human experience, such as emotion, beauty, and desire—which had been neglected in the dialogue with people who seemed to value rationale above all else—were ready to come cascading down the slope, dramatically reshaping the conversation.

One of the fastest-growing demographic categories today consists of those people who check "None" when asked to characterize their religious beliefs.[§] These "nones" are typically not committed atheists; they simply do not identify with any of the major established religions. Many of these people consider themselves spiritual and have historically been among the *most* likely to try out new spiritualities.[6] In other words, they are those who looked on during the debate between rational atheism and rational Christianity and found neither appealing, so they walked through door number three into whatever ambiguous, quasi-religious spirituality lay beyond.

The New Atheists' anti-religious rhetoric resonated with a segment of society that felt disenfranchised by religion. However, the worldview offered in its place was no more appealing. These atheists attempted to build a worldview with only one tool. Reason was useful for tearing down but was not adequate, on its own, to rebuild from the rubble. As Alister McGrath notes, "The New Atheism refuses to

---

§ The number of those who identify as religious "nones" (unaffiliated with any particular religion) has risen to approximately one in three adults in the United States. Gregory A. Smith, "About Three-in-Ten U.S. Adults Are Now Religiously Unaffiliated," Pew Research Center, December 14, 2021, www.pewresearch.org/religion/2021/12/14/about-three-in-ten-u-s-adults-are-now-religiously-unaffiliated/.

confront the inconvenient truth that every worldview—whether religious or secular—goes beyond what reason or science can prove."[7]

The cold rationality of atheism claimed to offer something *true*, but it was not *beautiful*. It spoke to the head but left the heart wanting. The New Atheists were blind to the rockslide. Could that be part of why they have lost much of their relevance in culture today?[¶]

Will the church suffer the same fate?

Question 2: What Is the New Paradigm?
The Aftermath

You have likely already gained an anecdotal understanding of the Heart Culture simply by looking at the rubble left in the wake of the cultural rockslide. But standing in the midst of something does not always afford the clearest vantage point to discern the big picture. So let's back up and define it.

We could say the mantra of the Head Culture is the famous saying of the philosopher Descartes, "I think, therefore I am." In a Heart Culture, it might be, "I *feel*, therefore I am." This does not mean that people today are more emotional in the sense of living in a perpetual state of blubbering tears (just as a Head Culture does not envision everyone as walking computers). You can be a macho guy who shrugs off emotional moments in a movie and yet still be a citizen of the Heart Culture. What the new mantra means is that internal feelings or affections have been elevated to the highest value and are the prime

---

¶ Interestingly, Sam Harris has shifted his focus to try to meet this need, writing *Waking Up: A Guide to Spirituality without Religion*, as well as launching a podcast of the same name. Richard Dawkins has also attempted to dip his toes into the Heart Culture by launching his own podcast, *The Poetry of Reality*.

motivator for action. What we feel *inside* ourselves determines how we interpret what is true *outside* ourselves and how we act upon that truth.

A keyboard warrior may be quick to jump into every political debate on social media armed with an endless barrage of rational arguments while simultaneously operating within an emotional narrative framework of good versus evil and heroes versus villains.

The emotionally distant "gym rat" may spend every morning pumping iron to add to a hard exterior while at the same time be motivated by insecurity about his body as the result of hurtful bullying in middle school.

A politician may make resisting the emotional excess of culture part of her campaign platform but then seek to stir up feelings of outrage to win over potential voters.

In his or her own way, each one is attempting to bring the reality outside him or herself into alignment with the internal sense of identity and truth he or she feels inside.

The cold rationality of atheism claimed to offer something *true*, but it was not *beautiful*. It spoke to the head but left the heart wanting.

Remember the man Daniel met at the conference in the opening story of this book? The irony of that encounter was that his denunciation of the emotion-driven culture was itself largely an emotional response. It was not a dispassionate calculation of data that drove him to arm himself with apologetic arguments. It was a love for young adults he knew personally and frustration at his own ineffectiveness to help them. Even as he condemned the Heart Culture, he was showing himself to be a citizen of it. If we're honest with ourselves, we will see throughout this book that the same is true of us.

When the evaluation of truth begins from the inside and works its way out, there are seismic implications for how people formulate belief systems and relate to others who do not share those values. Since we all experience the world in unique ways, *the* truth becomes replaced by a more individualistic "*my* truth." As a result, events that would have been unthinkable a few decades ago, such as a biological male being awarded "Woman of the Year,"[8] are not only possible but increasingly normalized, because the basis for identity is transplanted from shared objective standards into subjective individual feelings.

If rationality rules as king of a culture, then opposing ideologies are an invitation for debate and discussion on a fairly even playing field using the shared rules of logic, reason, and evidence. If emotionalism sits on the throne, then criticism is perceived as a challenge to personal identity and may even be considered "violence." Once truth becomes based on subjective feelings, then disagreement does not just make you wrong, it often makes you hateful, since you are not seen to be refuting an abstract idea but an individual person.

A Benevolent King of Hearts

In our current Heart Culture, negative examples of emotional excess are always easy to find and easily disseminated in a viral video or explosive article headline, but these do not tell the whole story. The negative expressions of the Heart Culture are akin to a stomachache we get after devouring a second piece of cheesecake, an unhealthy over-indulgence in something that, in moderation, is a good thing. After all, a society filled with emotionless cyborgs and calculating AI is the stuff of dystopian sci-fi, not an ideal to strive toward. The rediscovery of the heart has also led to much good.

Many young adults within the Heart Culture are more concerned with making a positive impact on the world than in climbing a corporate ladder. The younger Heart Culture citizens are challenging the status quo by seeking a healthier balance of work and family life than their parents may have had. They desire to invest their lives in fulfilling things they *love* rather than just putting in time doing what they are told they have to do. They are also more prone to question *why* something is the right thing to do rather than simply accepting what has always been the case.

For years, a culture of the head rationalized—or ignored—the open secret of sexual abuse, until a culture of the heart faced it head on in the #MeToo movement. The emotionally driven Heart Culture of today is one that cares with a white-hot passion for justice, inclusion, and equality. What these values look like and how they are best achieved can be debated, but heart people's desire for them often arises from a place of genuine care and love for others.

In the movie *Dead Poets Society*, Robin Williams's character gives a monologue about poetry that reflects what a Heart Culture (at its best) strives toward:

> We don't read and write poetry because it's cute. We
> read and write poetry because we are members of
> the human race. And the human race is filled with

passion. And medicine, law, business, engineering, these are noble pursuits and necessary to sustain life. But poetry, beauty, romance, love, these are what we stay alive for.[9]

A society filled with only poets would quickly crumble, but a society built on logic alone, while functional, would grow intolerable. Although it is prone to excess, the Heart Culture has reaffirmed the emotions and desires that make us human.

For better or worse, it is increasingly clear that we have moved from a Head to a Heart Culture. While stones and pebbles continue to trickle down the slope, we live in the aftermath of the rockslide. The terrain has changed. How will we respond?

Question 3: How Do We Respond?
Life Amid the Rubble

An emphasis on the head helped Christians effectively engage with the New Atheism of yesterday, but it was never meant to be a one-size-fits-all template. Just as Nunez's willing "blindness" allowed him to relate to the blind but not spot the rockslide, Christians must open their eyes to the new paradigm.

We remember seeing this question broadcast out on social media by a notable Christian Hollywood celebrity: "If Darwin was right, then why are there still monkeys?" It was immediately met with mockery by Darwinists but also, perhaps surprisingly, by Christians. The ridicule stemmed not just from the celebrity's misunderstanding of Darwin's theory but also because the argument had the unpleasant aroma of "an oldie but a goodie" rather than a contemporary contribution to an ongoing discussion.

Debates about creation and evolution once dominated the discourse, but such issues are no longer at the forefront of apologetics. They are still important questions but are not the primary ones the culture is asking.

Instead, today it is more common to hear skeptics make declarations like, "I can't believe in a God who would _____." That blank can be filled with any number of statements, from "send unbelievers to hell" to "condemn the LGBTQ+ community." It's an emotional objection rather than a rational one, since the existence of something does not depend on what we might *feel* toward it. (Our wives might claim they can't believe in intelligent human life that would dip their grilled cheese in ketchup, and yet here we are!)

People who are convinced that God is a vengeful, intolerant, unloving deity who stands against the values they hold in highest regard are unmotivated to investigate whether He exists or not. The Heart Culture rejects the notion that the Christian gospel is "good news" not because they question whether the news is factual, but because they doubt whether it is "good." As agnostic philosopher Thomas Nagel once wrote: "It isn't just that I don't believe in God and, naturally, hope that I'm right in my belief. It's that I hope there is no God! I don't want there to be a God; I don't want the universe to be like that."[10]

Skeptics outside the church, along with those leaving the church and those merely apathetic or disengaged from the faith, are not primarily wrestling with the idea that God is *irrational* but with the notion that God is *good*. Objections of the heart, not of the head.

Sliding Into the Church (and Out the Back Door)

The rockslide has not remained on the periphery of the village. It has rolled into our churches and carried many Christians with it out the back door.

The image of the atheist college professor bulldozing sheltered Christian freshmen out of their faith remains poignant and ingrained in the minds of many, but data suggests that these fears are overblown. When surveyed, almost none of the prodigals (those who left their Christian faith after high school) responded that their spiritual wandering was inspired by encountering new rational arguments or data. Most simply got bored. They did not necessarily struggle with doctrine or factual evidence but lost *attraction* to the Christian faith. A recent survey found that 71 percent of those who left didn't do so intentionally; they just drifted and replaced church with something else.[11]

When these prodigals do voice objections, they sound like the criticisms given by the wider secular culture. David Kinnaman (Barna Research) identifies six key reasons why young people are leaving religious institutions. They perceive the church as:

- **Overprotective** (doesn't allow for creative expression or innovation)
- **Shallow** (church is boring)
- **Antiscience** (can't keep up with scientific breakthroughs of today)
- **Repressive** (specifically in its sexual ethics)
- **Exclusive** (not open-minded or tolerant)
- **Doubtless** (does not encourage healthy skepticism or questioning).[12]

With the possible exception of number three, these issues arise from an *emotional* place. The church, for all its efforts to reach young people, is not properly engaging their creative and emotional side. We are still operating within the framework of a Head Culture, depositing biblical knowledge into their minds several times a week but leaving their hearts empty.

Deconstructing the Christian Head

Another trend in the Heart Culture is a growing movement called *deconstruction*. The movement is complex and sometimes misrepresented, leading to either a spiritually edifying or a spiritually destructive end, depending on the individual. In many ways, deconstruction is a response to negative perceptions of the church. The movement has not been driven by rational disagreement as much as by a heart response to unpleasant or painful experiences within the church.

As the #MeToo movement expanded into #ChurchToo, many high-profile Christian leaders were exposed as sexual or emotional abusers and hypocrites. The response of the church to cultural issues has not always been "with gentleness and respect" (1 Pet. 3:15), and people have noticed. Many who grew up within unhealthy church environments have begun a process of sifting through what the Bible says, what they have always been told, and what they feel in their hearts to be true. Such a journey of deconstruction can begin with visceral responses to institutions that often rationalized abusive behavior.

Kinnaman distinguishes between head-driven prodigals and heart-driven prodigals:

Frequently head-driven prodigals define themselves by their new faith choices, while heart-driven prodigals focus on their denunciation of Christianity. There also seems to be something open-ended and unresolved about heart-driven prodigals, as though their spiritual flame could reignite at any moment; head-driven prodigals, by contrast, seem to be more settled in, perhaps even resigned to, their distance from the faith.[13]

Those driven by the heart provide an incredible redemptive opportunity for the church if we have eyes to see it.

Eyes Were Made to See

As we look at the rubble deposited all around us by the Heart Culture rockslide, it is understandable that many Christians yearn for a time when things were different. We long for what is comfortable and familiar, and the debris scattered across our path is intimidating. We see the extreme manifestations of an emotionally driven culture and become frustrated (ironically, a heart response). But there *is* a way forward.

In *The Country of the Blind*, Nunez's success in navigating the new challenge began by rediscovering his eyes and the revelation that sight is a beautiful and valuable force. Accommodating the blind was necessary in the moment, but it never represented a full picture of reality.

Will we in the church willingly gouge out our eyes to avoid dealing with uncomfortable sights, choosing self-imposed blindness even as the rocks tumble down around us? Or will the emergent Heart Culture inspire us to discover an important truth about ourselves—that the same eyes can look upon both the grotesque *and* the beautiful? More importantly, they can find beauty *in* the seemingly ugly.

As we gaze at the mountains and recall the good things that lay beyond, we will discover that the dominance of the heart over the head is not just true of our culture, it is true of *us*. God has created each of us as thinkers and feelers, beings with a union between reason and affections. Our hearts and our minds find their ultimate fulfillment in the Creator.

Jesus once lamented, "For this people's heart has become calloused; they hardly hear with their ears, and they have closed their eyes. Otherwise they might see with their eyes, hear with their ears, understand with their hearts and turn, and I would heal them" (Matt. 13:15). May God open our eyes so He might heal our hearts.

Chapter 2

The Rational Irrationality
of Heart People

We cannot reason ourselves out of our basic irrationality.
All we can do is to learn the art of being irrational in a reasonable way.

—Old Raja in *Island*, Aldous Huxley

One ought to hold on to one's heart;
for if one lets it go, one soon loses control of the head too.

—Friedrich Nietzsche

The "It" Factor

.609 OBP, 11.9 WAR, .812 SLG, .537 wOBA.

No, these numbers are not complex rocket launch trajectory data from NASA. If you're a sports nerd, you probably recognize them. They are an analytical breakdown of Major League Baseball superstar Barry Bonds's 2004 season, arguably the greatest season in league history.

Notably, this was *not* the season when he rewrote the cherished home run record with seventy-three.* As sports became more data

---

* Yes, you can put an asterisk there if you want.

driven, analyzing greatness evolved into something more nuanced than, "He hit lots of balls out of the park. That seems good." This data-driven movement, brought to widespread attention by the movie *Moneyball*, has now spread to all corners of the sporting world.

What might be overlooked in the meteoric rise of sports analytics is the fact that the "moneyball" Oakland Athletics never won a championship. Also, despite that sublime analytic season, Barry Bonds has not yet made it into the Baseball Hall of Fame due to accusations of performance-enhancing drug use and a soiled reputation.

Statistics and data are valuable, but they don't tell the whole story. As Michael Jordan tells the Looney Toons characters in *Space Jam*, "You got a lot of ... a lot of .... Well, whatever it is, you got a lot of it."[1]

That unquantifiable "it" factor resists statistical analysis because it derives from the heart. There is a reason why most sports movies have an impassioned locker-room speech scene to inspire the underdogs to victory rather than a fourth-quarter algorithm assessment! No story involving humans can ever be reduced to data and numbers, because humans are complex, self-contradicting, messy "heart people."

In the previous chapter, we explored the rockslide of the Heart Culture. Societal values and norms may have shifted, giving superiority to subjective feelings, but humans did not wake up one day and discover their affections. We have *always* been "heart people." To effectively engage with today's Heart Culture, we must recognize that we too are products of and contributors to that very culture. In the next chapter, we will explore how to speak the language of the Heart Culture. Before we get there, we must first recognize that the language of the heart is not some foreign dialect; it is our native tongue.

Complex Creatures

There is arguably no more relatable statement in the Bible than the apostle Paul's lament: "I do not understand what I do. For what I want to do I do not do, but what I hate I do" (Rom. 7:15). Anyone who has set an ambitious New Year's resolution to get healthier but then noticed some delicious leftover Christmas cookies on the counter can surely relate!

We are reminded of our respectable father who one time *licked* a seemingly ineffective phone charger ... while it was plugged into the wall ... to find out if it was conducting electricity. With hair standing on end and a smoking tongue, he felt the need to tell his concerned family, "Don't worry, I have a PhD!"[†]

Humans are complex creatures. We are living paradoxes, messy concoctions of thoughts and feelings that don't always exist in perfect harmony and are often difficult to disentangle and understand. Psychologist Jonathan Haidt observes, "One of the greatest truths of psychology is that the mind is divided into parts that sometimes conflict."[2]

Over the last several decades, psychologists have repeatedly affirmed that humans are—for better or worse—fundamentally emotional beings. As infants, we begin our pilgrimage through the world as emotional creatures, crying to indicate needs we do not understand or have the ability to articulate. Only as we grow and mature do we develop our rational minds (with men, on average, taking longer to develop than women!). Still, that emotional foundation remains rooted within us. Our newfound rationality does not replace our

---

† In history, not electrical engineering.

primal emotionalism; it merely allows us to harness and direct it, with varying degrees of success.

Psychologists may be confirming it for today's audiences, but this truth has long been part of ancient wisdom. Proverbs 4:23 cautions us, "Above all else, guard your heart, for everything you do flows from it." Biblically, the heart is "deceitful above all things" (Jer. 17:9), and yet when Jesus affirms the first and greatest command, the heart is given a position of great importance: "Love the Lord your God with all your *heart*" (Matt. 22:37). The heart has the power to lead us into proper worship of God or into destructive sin, which is why understanding the workings of the heart is crucial.

Our best poets have spent centuries probing the mysteries of the heart, yet the code remains decisively uncracked. What follows is far from exhaustive, but there are at least three important realities about the relationship between heart and head that are foundational for everything that follows.

Three Realities of Heart and Head
Reality 1: We Are Rational and Emotional

One of the most popular metaphorical frameworks of the head/heart duality is the idea of being right-brained or left-brained. The metaphor is based on the work of neuropsychologist Roger Wolcott Sperry, who was awarded the 1981 Nobel Prize in Science and Medicine for his split-brain research and contribution to the current understanding of the lateralization of brain function. He, and many others, discovered that different sections of the brain are specialized for particular tasks.

As the theory goes, those with a dominant left hemisphere of the brain are more analytical and rational (head people), while the right-brained among us are the more creative and intuitive (heart people). As a metaphor, the distinction is helpful to categorize and understand how certain individuals tick. It is not uncommon in primary school for students to be shown visual depictions of the split brain—the left filled with numbers and equations, the right with rainbows of bright colors—and asked to identify themselves.

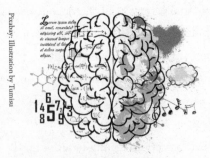

Pixabay: Illustration by Tumisu

Left brain/right brain concept

Nevertheless, the left/right metaphor was never a good fit for what the science was showing. Every person, the mathematician and the artist alike, has two hemispheres in his or her brain. The popular metaphor is partially responsible for setting rationality and emotion in opposition to each other.

The two of us are brothers. We are often perceived as opposites, with Mike labeled the "thinker" and Daniel the "feeler." The truth is that we're each a mixture of both. We may identify more with one hemisphere, but the other is actively functioning as well.

The same is true of the culture at large. While head or heart may be given more attention and authority than the other, a culture is never exclusively one or the other. In God's perfect design, He created humans with a full brain. An individual person—or a society full of people—who attempts to create a schism between the two is living contrary to our created nature. We may put more emphasis on one over the other (and our culture will reflect that preference), but they both always exist in tandem.

Learning the language of the heart is not just a tactic to communicate with the romantic artists and the so-called "sensitive" folks in the world, it is a language that *all* people speak with varying degrees of fluidity.

In *Harry Potter and the Order of the Phoenix*, there is an amusing scene in which Hermione tries to explain to Harry all the discordant emotions that Cho (his romantic crush) is currently experiencing. Their friend Ron chimes in, "One person can't feel all that at once, they'd explode." To which a frustrated Hermione responds, "Just because you've got the emotional range of a teaspoon doesn't mean we all have!"[3] What's interesting about the exchange is that Hermione is arguably the most rational of them all, and Ron perhaps the most emotional. It's not that Ron doesn't *have* emotions, it's that they often manifest themselves differently and he is less adept at processing and articulating them.

You may not consider yourself an emotional person. To be clear: we are not using "heart" as a synonym for "emotion" but to refer to a deep impulse that drives us at an often subconscious level. Those who "wear their emotions on their sleeves" may be easier to pinpoint as heart people, and yet it may be that their passions manifest in more outwardly expressive ways or that they are more fluent at speaking the *language* of the heart. Deep down, even the most logical among us are driven by the heart; it may just be less obvious from the outside.

Reality 2: We're Not as Rational as We Think We Are

The great Italian poet Dante Alighieri declared, "Man alone amongst the animals speaks and has gestures and expression which we call rational, because he alone has reason in him."[4] Reason is one of the defining traits of humanity, and one that many people take great pride in. Yet, in an ironic turn of events, the most rational-minded people among us, psychologists and scientists, have discovered that we are actually not as rational as we *think* we are. Thus, in what is itself an amusing picture of human complexity, we have poets arguing for our rationality and scientists asserting our emotionality!

According to much research, rather than beings that always make rational decisions, humans are more often driven by our emotions. It is not just that we operate with both emotion and reason, but that emotion is actually most often in the driver's seat. For example, when it comes to making decisions about right and wrong, the typical response is to decide what we think based on our emotional intuition (what we "feel") and then use our reasoning capabilities to *justify* the decision we've already come to (what we "think").

Referring to one of many experiments testing this, psychologist Jonathan Haidt writes, "People made moral judgements quickly and emotionally. Moral reasoning was mostly just a post hoc search for reasons to justify the judgments people had already made."[5] Whether we realize it or not, we are not so much interested in finding the truth of a situation as we are in coming up with an explanation that makes sense to us ("*my* truth"). Like an agenda-driven news outlet, we start with the narrative we want to present and then selectively search for the facts, evidence, and testimony to support it (a phenomenon called "confirmation bias").[6]

As a result, it is hard to change someone's mind once he has settled on what he *feels* to be true and has furnished his conviction with rational justifications to legitimize it. Discussions and debates rarely involve people actually considering opposing information. Rather, it is often an attempt to prop up one's own view in the face of the new information offered. This is why debates rarely lead people to new positions. In fact, research even suggests that the *smarter* you are, the *harder* it is to update your beliefs.[7]

The comedian Brian Regan sarcastically notes, "Hey, I saw something interesting today on social media. Somebody posted a very strong political opinion. And somebody replied, 'Good point. I changed my mind.'" He quickly follows up with, "No, I'm sorry. I saw a unicorn. I saw a unicorn. I saw a purple glittery flying unicorn."[8]

Interestingly, humans use different processes for *judgment* and *justification*. We make up our minds about situations based on intuition, but when asked to explain how we came to our conclusions, we don't actually know! We typically try to come up with a rational explanation for how we developed our beliefs, but our initial judgments were not actually the result of careful reasoning.[9] In other words, we make judgments from the heart, but feel as though we owe others a "head" explanation.

For example, if someone tells you a story involving incest, your immediate reaction is (hopefully) "That is so wrong." If asked *why* you think it's wrong, you can likely come up with various reasons. But those reasons were thought of *after* your initial reaction. Even if a clever philosopher were to respond to your reasons with clever counterpoints, it still would not change how you *felt* about the situation.

In short, it seems that we are not rational creatures with emotions, but emotional creatures with the capacity for reason.

Reality 3: Head and Heart Are Allies, Not Enemies

The original *Star Trek* science fiction series explored the head and heart relationship by embodying it in a yin-yang dynamic between characters Spock (the rational one) and McCoy (the passionate one). The dynamic worked precisely because each character represented half of a whole. In order to complete missions, Captain Kirk needed to find the balance between them because neither the passionate emotionality of McCoy nor the analytic logic of Spock were sufficient to navigate the situation alone.

Other famous duos have been built on a similar premise, such as the sisters who represent both sides of Jane Austen's novel *Sense and Sensibility* or Sir Arthur Conan Doyle's character John Watson, whose empathy balanced Sherlock Holmes's shrewd deductions.

In Reality One, we observed that every person is a mixture of head and heart, and in Reality Two, we saw that the heart is typically the more influential of the two. While head and heart sometimes conflict, this does not mean they're pitted against each other as enemies. In fact, together they help us navigate the myriad choices we make every day, with emotion assigning value to things, and reason then choosing between the available options.[10]

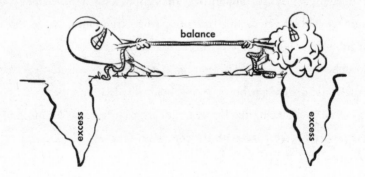

We can imagine the dynamic as an inverted game of tug-of-war. Head and heart are both pulling on the rope, only instead of a pit existing in the middle between them, chasms exist *behind* both participants. Unlike regular tug-of-war, the objective is not to pull the opponent into the middle pit but for each team to prevent the other from pulling itself into the chasm behind them. When working together, both pulling in equal measure, there is balance.

Many classic stories have explored the disaster that arises when this equilibrium is broken. Miguel de Cervantes's *Don Quixote*, often considered the first modern novel, tells of a man with a head so stuffed full of romances and tales of chivalry that he loses his mind and finds himself jousting with windmills, having mistaken them for evil giants. A man with a beating heart but not a thinking head becomes a tragic comedy.

Wikimedia Commons: Illustration by G. A. Harker

Don Quixote fighting windmills

Charles Dickens's *Hard Times* explores the opposite. The novel begins with a grouchy schoolmaster declaring, "Now, what I want is, Facts. Teach these boys and girls nothing but Facts. Facts alone are wanted in life. Plant nothing else, and root out everything else. You can only form the minds of reasoning animals upon Facts: nothing else will ever be of any service to them."[11] The story then illustrates how such an education has left the students impoverished and unable to cope in their world. As the students grow as people with heads but no hearts, they grieve their lost humanity.

It seems that we are not rational creatures
with emotions, but emotional creatures
with the capacity for reason.

Unfortunately, the reality that either the head or the heart could tumble into the chasm is not restricted to novels. We have witnessed doomed relationships in real life where the couple ignored wise counsel in order to follow their hearts into an ill-suited marriage, resulting in brokenness.

On the other hand, we can sometimes feel an intuitive stirring in our hearts toward a certain action, only to slowly rationalize those feelings away. We knew someone who felt moved to reach out to a classmate who seemed unsettled, but he quickly rationalized himself out of it. After all, they really weren't that close of friends, and someone else would probably be better at helping him. So he did nothing. Later that week, he was met with the news that his classmate had committed suicide. His heart had sensed a need, but his head had rationalized it away.

The apostle Paul put it this way: "If I speak in the tongues of men or of angels, but do not have love, I am only a resounding gong or a clanging cymbal. If I have the gift of prophecy and can fathom all mysteries and all knowledge, and if I have a faith that can move mountains, but do not have love, I am nothing" (1 Cor. 13:1–2). The head keeps the heart in check, but the chasm that exists behind the head is no less treacherous should the heart release the rope.

The Power of a Good Cinematic Experience

If we are a paradox of rational irrationality, then how are the seemingly polarized head and heart supposed to work together? Perhaps we can find answers where we often discover truths about life—at the movies.

We may not measure a Fast & Furious flick against van Gogh's *Starry Night Over the Rhône* or include Michael Bay alongside Mozart, but at its best, cinema may be the most powerful art form of them all. Cinema incorporates all the other artistic vehicles into a single, potent experience. A film is narrative but also a deeply sensory medium that blends music with visuals. Every time you sit in a movie theater, the experience involves seeing, hearing, and (hopefully) thinking.[‡] There is simply no aesthetic experience like cinema. Consider the following:

Starry Night Over the Rhone

Wikimedia Commons: Painting by Vincent van Gogh

Dunnnn dun. Dunnnn dun. Dunnn dun dunnn dun dunn dun dun dun ...

What comes to mind? You win if you recognized these words as the famous John Williams theme from Steven Spielberg's classic blockbuster, *Jaws*. Today (at least for viewers of a certain age), the iconic theme, with ominously alternating notes between E and F, instantly produces feelings of unease. But that was not always the case. When

---

‡ Feel free to also include "tasting," since no theater experience is complete without Reese's Pieces.

Williams first played the song to Spielberg, the bewildered director declared, "You can't be serious!"[12] The music didn't seem scary enough.

But when paired with the narrative framework of a man-eating shark prowling the coast of Amity Island, those E and F notes took on a whole new meaning. Now those two notes evoke fear and unease, not necessarily because the music itself is unsettling, but because of what it arouses in our imaginations.

On the other hand, you may not know that *Jaws* was originally a novel by Peter Benchley. The book was popular, but it did not instill a generation of people with a traumatic fear of the water as the movie did. Both the novel and the film tell a story about a dangerous shark, but the film conveys the story through multiple senses ("Dunnnn dun. Dunnnn dun ...") in such an immersive way that five decades later the popular Shark Week programming on the Discovery Channel is still trying to combat those fears and change the narrative.

A great film works because its narrative framework gives meaning to the emotional and sensory experience, while those sensory elements simultaneously infuse power and potency into that narrative framework.[13] The result is a satisfying overall experience that has become a staple in society and one of the most profitable industries in the world.§

Life like the Movies

The cinematic experience is an example of how we are designed to process the world as creatures of head and heart. Our rational minds are akin to the narrative structure of a film. The head makes sense of

---

§ Not only does film music make audiences feel something, it also guides them on *what* to feel by providing auditory cues that allow audiences to more clearly interpret the story they are witnessing.

our feelings. Without a rational framework to provide structure, our feelings become aimless. Such is often on display in our current Heart Culture, as heart citizens are violently swept back and forth on the winds of their ever-changing whims.

Conversely, it is our hearts that provide vibrancy to the worldview structures of our heads. When you read the Wikipedia plot summary for *Jaws*, your pulse is unlikely to quicken. There is a dramatic difference between *knowing* something at a factual level and fully *experiencing* it.

The same is true of the Christian faith. As the church seeks to communicate the gospel of Jesus to a Heart Culture, we must offer more than a Wikipedia plot summary. A distilled outline may be 100 percent factually accurate but fail to stir someone's emotions. That's because this story was never intended to be merely a plot sketch. It was designed by the master Storyteller to be an immersive, emotionally satisfying experience.

If the wider Heart Culture has been guilty of offering music detached from a proper narrative to give it meaning, then perhaps the church might be accused of presenting a plot summary without the soundtrack. The remainder of this book is about how to incorporate that musical score. To focus on the aesthetic elements that resonate with the heart does not diminish the importance of the plot. On the contrary, these elements allow people to experience the gospel in all its vibrant fullness.

Conclusion

We are beautifully complex creatures. We may watch aghast at the emotionalism in the world around us, but a look inside our own hearts should be enough to prevent us from casting stones of condemnation. We too are emotional creatures—and that is good news because we experience many of the best parts of our lives in these messy emotions.

Our ability to reason sets us apart in the animal kingdom, but at our core, we are all heart people. It is in these shared concerns of the heart that we find common ground with those inside and outside our churches. The gospel has always been good news delivered to the head *and* heart, and our Heart Culture longs to experience it.

Chapter 3

Straight to the Heart

Hamlet: .... There are more things in heaven and Earth, Horatio,
than are dreamt of in your philosophy.

—William Shakespeare, *Hamlet*

Jesus is a teacher who doesn't just inform our
intellect but forms our very loves.

—James K. A. Smith

Culture Shapers

In the early 1900s, five uneducated immigrants came to America—
and changed it forever. As outsiders without social power or influence,
they encountered closed doors at every turn. These five men did not
yet know each other, but their destinies would become entwined, for
they shared a driving conviction: if the country did not have a place for
them, they would simply need to remake the country. Their paths were
unique, but each ultimately gravitated toward the same instrument to
do so: motion pictures.

These five men would go on to pioneer the legendary movie studios: Universal Pictures, Paramount Pictures, Fox Film Corporation,
Metro-Goldwyn-Mayer (MGM), and Warner Brothers. Through

their films, they enticed the culture with a new vision for the country. As one biographer aptly writes, "[They] created a powerful cluster of images and ideas—so powerful that, in a sense, they colonized the American imagination."[1]

These five, our first movie moguls, harnessed story and visuals in a way that spoke to the hearts of audiences to such a degree that the world of today has largely come to reflect the image of it they built through Hollywood. "What remains is a spell, a landscape of the mind, a constellation of values, attitudes, and images, a history and a mythology that is part of our culture and our consciousness. What remains is the America of our imaginations and theirs."[2]

Journeying Upstream

Hollywood's origin story is a fascinating underdog tale about appealing to imagination in order to reshape a culture. Like many storylines arising from Tinseltown, its own plot is not wholly original. The eighteenth-century Scottish politician Andrew Fletcher declared, "If a man were permitted to make all the Ballads, he need not care who should make the Laws of a Nation. And we find that most of the ancient Legislators thought they could not well reform the manners of any City without the help of a Lyric, and sometimes of a Dramatic Poet."[3] That is why in Plato's *Republic*, when he casts a vision for the utopian state, the great philosopher spends just one paragraph on money and economics and nearly thirty pages on music and what we might call matters of the heart.[4]

From the ancient civilizations, to the golden age of Hollywood, until today, there has always been a sense that the most fruitful path to influencing the world is by appealing to the *heart*.

There is a popular saying: "Politics is downstream of culture." For our purposes, we might adapt this mantra to: "The head is downstream of the heart." The heart is the source of the river, and "everything you do flows from it" (Prov. 4:23). As "fishers of men" (Matt. 4:19 ESV), we can become too comfortable standing downstream, dipping into the countless tributaries or water channels that branch off from the tumultuous river. We scramble to respond to the outward expression of ideologies and worldviews but feel powerless against the raging current of the river. As the church, we may desperately *want* to influence our culture as Jesus has called us to but are bewildered at how to do so effectively.

In the previous chapters, we established that we are all fundamentally heart people living in a Heart Culture. If this is true, then the most effective approach will be one that goes right to the source of the river. This is not an attempt to discover a new gimmick to try to make the church appear relevant to the world. It is a deep realization that who we are and how we relate to each other and to God has always been rooted in the language of the heart.

In this chapter, we will discover what it looks like to journey upstream toward the source of that river. What we will find there is a God who appeals to our heart's deepest desires for story, beauty, and wonder.

God Speaks the Language of the Heart

We don't know God automatically. We may have an innate desire to know Him, but *His* initiative and revelation invites us into that relationship (John 6:44). How God has chosen to communicate about

Himself can teach us much about how we can communicate to others about Him.

The Bible is the cornerstone for our understanding of God. We may view Scripture as mainly a "head" appeal—as information we deposit into our brains. However, in both the message (*what* is communicated) and the medium (*how* it is communicated), we discover that the Bible continually appeals to the heart.

The original audience would have understood the heart in a more holistic manner than we do today. They would've thought of it not just as "emotional feelings" but as the core of who we are. The word "heart" is used more than eight hundred times in English translations of the Bible, while "mind" appears fewer than one hundred times.* Within the pages of Scripture, we encounter narrative, poetry, song, metaphor, and a God who delights in using heart language to relate to people. Let us examine five ways.

1. A God of Beauty

Both times in the Old Testament when a dwelling was built for God, He took a surprisingly active role in the process as architect and interior designer. God provided Moses with a specific blueprint for the tabernacle (Ex. 25:9, 40), and later inspired the layout of the temple (1 Chron. 28:12, 19). The Bible contains page after page of detailed descriptions of those plans—chapters we may be tempted to skip. These summaries provide a glimpse into the heart of a God who values art and beauty, not just functionality.

---

* These numbers come from *Strong's Exhaustive Concordance of the Bible*, in regard to the King James Version of the Bible.

The temple was home to a diverse range of artistic styles, including symbolic, representational, and abstract.[5] Even the Most Holy Place, entered only once a year by only one person (the high priest), contained the majestic art of two golden cherubim sculptures. While many of the aesthetic elements served a religious or symbolic purpose, not all did. Freestanding pillars bore artistic adornment but no structural burden, and precious stones were included "for beauty" (2 Chron. 3:6 KJV).

When Scripture describes God, it is often through the language of beauty. Psalm 27:4 says, "One thing I ask from the LORD, this only do I seek: that I may dwell in the house of the LORD all the days of my life, to gaze on the *beauty* of the LORD and to seek him in his temple." God is all-powerful, all-knowing, and perfectly loving, but Scripture also reminds us of His beauty.

2. A God of Music and Poetry

Throughout the Bible, people make music in response to God's presence. The heavenly throne room is a hall of music and song (Rev. 5). When God inspired His special revelation through Scripture, He arranged that the largest book contained in the library would be the Psalms, which is a collection of songs and poetry.

While cultural distance and the translation process may make it difficult for present-day readers to recognize this, scholars have estimated that as much as 33 percent of the Bible could be considered poetic.[6] Even the prophets, when bringing messages of doom and destruction from God, often used poetic language (like ancient heavy metal singers)! What does it say about God that our canon of Scripture omits any extended intellectual discourse on the doctrine of the Holy Trinity but includes the Song of Songs, a book full of sensual poetry?

3. A God of Captivating Stories

Another revealing aspect of the Bible is the elevation of story. Narrative is the most common type of literature in the Bible, constituting more than 40 percent of the Old Testament and much of the New Testament.[7] As God revealed Himself to the Israelite people in the Old Testament, they were encouraged to pass on the stories so future generations would come to know Him as they had (see Ex. 12:25-27; Josh. 4:19–24; Ps. 145:4). The ancient cultures were largely oral, preserving their history through spoken stories more than writing. The gospel accounts of Jesus were shared orally before they were written down into what we read today.

During Jesus' earthly ministry, He demonstrated this storytelling nature: "Jesus spoke all these things to the crowd in parables; he did not say anything to them without using a parable" (Matt. 13:34). When seeking to communicate the spiritual realities of His coming kingdom and the abundant life He offered, Jesus repeatedly found stories to be the most effective vehicle to do so.

4. A God of Metaphors and Symbolism

In one of the most mystifying moments in the Bible, when Jesus exhaled His final breath on the cross, the sky darkened. Nature itself became the canvas for God's artistry, and the veil of the temple was miraculously torn in two (Matt. 27:51; Mark 15:38; Luke 23:45). The veil had separated the holy (God) from the profane (people). Christ's death removed the spiritual veil, and God provided a tangible metaphor to illustrate the significance of that moment.

Metaphors are a crucial way that God reveals His nature to us. Rebecca McLaughlin writes, "From a Christian perspective, metaphor is vital to theology: without it, we cannot hope to describe the invisible, transcendent, ungraspable God."[8] Jesus often used word pictures to reveal important realities. In explaining the kingdom of God, He repeatedly used the language of metaphor ("You *are* the light of the world ..." [Matt. 5:14]) and simile ("... the kingdom of God is *like* ..." [Mark 4:26]).

In fact, the gospel itself is largely predicated on such imagery: "The Word became flesh and made his dwelling among us. We have seen his glory, the glory of the one and only Son, who came from the Father, full of grace and truth" (John 1:14). In the incarnation, Jesus became the "image of the invisible God" (Col. 1:15). As the Son of God, Jesus was more than a metaphor, but the same function that makes metaphors powerful was evident in Him: making the abstract tangible and turning invisible realities into visible pictures.

Against this backdrop, it is unsurprising that the two acts Jesus instituted for His followers to practice, the Lord's Supper and baptism, are symbolic in nature. The wine and bread become representations of His blood and broken body, while baptism is a sort of drama, a symbolic picture of spiritual "new birth" (another metaphor from Jesus). They both give powerful visual representation to spiritual realities.

5. A God Who Satisfies Desires and Needs

The psalmist declared, "Take delight in the LORD, and he will give you the desires of your heart" (Ps. 37:4). Our hearts are full of longings, and they are met in relationship with our Creator: "As the deer pants for streams of water, so my soul pants for you, my God" (Ps. 42:1).

Through another simile, the lyrics capture the reality that our souls contain an unquenchable thirst for the divine. Jesus would later use similar language when He claimed, "I am the bread of life. He who comes to Me shall never hunger, and he who believes in Me shall never thirst" (John 6:35 NKJV).

Christ made those profound statements shortly after miraculously feeding the five thousand (vv. 1–14) and in the context of being questioned about God providing manna for the Israelites in the wilderness (vv. 30–31). As Jesus proclaimed the coming kingdom, He repeatedly used physical need and desire as a mirror to reflect internal spiritual yearnings for love, identity, purpose, and transcendence. He would take a similar approach in His implementation of the Lord's Supper. Just as our bodies desire food and water to satisfy our basic needs, so too are our spirits driven to pursue heart longings that only Jesus can satisfy.

The apostle John declares that love—the ultimate desire of the heart—finds its origin and definition within the character of God: "Everyone who loves has been born of God and knows God. Whoever does not love does not know God, because God is love" (1 John 4:7b–8). All throughout His ministry, Jesus presented Himself as the unlooked-for answer for deep, unquenchable spiritual needs that could not be satisfied outside of Him.

Heart Language 101

What is clear in these examples and many others is that God repeatedly revealed Himself through the language of the heart. Notice that God used methods related to the heart but also revealed Himself as a Being who resonates with the deepest yearning *of* our hearts. It is not just the language used to communicate the gospel message but is central to the message itself.

God did not use song and poetry merely as a technique to grab attention—the way a pastor may start off his sermon with a joke. Instead, it seems there are aspects of His person and ways that are best communicated through the imagination.

We operate under the same understanding with church worship. Congregations could solemnly read the words of the songs as an act of worship, but there is something more fitting about expressing them through song and infusing the words with melodies and harmonies.

Not all aspects of God are best communicated through aesthetic means; sermons need not resemble a Broadway musical! Nevertheless, even the more rational elements of our services are typically preceded or followed by music. We seem to intuitively understand that truths about God cannot be fully communicated, understood, or acted upon without speaking to the heart.

Putting Heart Language into Practice

The language of the heart is the *lingua franca* of our culture and of our species. It is a shared language that crosses boundaries and unites us. Learning to communicate using this vocabulary is not a way to give the gospel a flashy PR spin. The need goes further than that. The heart is how we understand a gospel that is true, good, *and* beautiful.

In a Heart Culture, to not be fluent in this language is to put ourselves at a serious disadvantage. Some of us may speak these dialects more fluently than others, but it is a language we all understand when we hear it. When children learn to talk, they understand speech before they can articulate a reply using their own voices. As children of

God, we have heard this language spoken to us by our heavenly Father. Comprehension comes through experience, but we master speaking through practice.

Let's look at a biblical example.

When in Athens

A biblical narrative in Acts 17 provides a helpful model for how we can speak the heart language to others:

> While Paul was waiting for them in Athens, he was greatly distressed to see that the city was full of idols. (v. 16)

Like Christians today, Paul gazed at the culture and was troubled. His surroundings provoked an emotional response in his spirit. Rather than bemoan what he saw, he took the opportunity to step in and engage with it. Notice how he begins his presentation:

> People of Athens! I see that in every way you are very religious. For as I walked around and looked carefully at your objects of worship, I even found an altar with this inscription: TO AN UNKNOWN GOD. So you are ignorant of the very thing you worship—and this is what I am going to proclaim to you. (vv. 22b–23)

Before speaking, Paul had spent time observing the surrounding artistry to understand his audience, gaining insight from the physical sculptures and aesthetic creations on display. His discourse is a direct response to the "why" of the sculptures, not just the "what" of the idols

themselves. Next, he appeals winsomely to their shared value of worship. Rather than mock what he sees as false, he finds common ground. Lastly, he gives an appeal to their sense of wonder and curiosity in the face of the mysterious.

St. Paul Preaching in Athens

Wikimedia Commons: Painting by Raphael

In this short introduction, Paul speaks to the hearts of his audience in three distinct ways: what they've made, who they are, and what they yearn for. While his presentation will also include logic and rational elements, he *begins* by activating their hearts.

To support his gospel claims, Paul also turns to the popular art of the day and quotes from two Greek poems (v. 28). The refrain "For in you we live and move and have our being" comes from the poem "Cretica" by Epimenides:

> They fashioned a tomb for you, holy and high one,
> Cretans, always liars, evil beasts, idle bellies.†
> But you are not dead: you live and abide forever,
> For in you we live and move and have our being.[9]

The quote, "For we are indeed his offspring," derives from "Phaenomena" by Aratus:

---

† Eagle-eyed Bible readers may also recognize that this same refrain gets quoted in Titus 1:12. ("One of Crete's own prophets has said it: 'Cretans are always liars, evil brutes, lazy gluttons.'")

Let us begin with Zeus, whom we mortals never leave
   unspoken.
For every street, every market-place is full of god.
Even the sea and the harbour are full of this deity.
Everywhere everyone is indebted to god.
For we are indeed his offspring.[10]

Paul is not merely jazzing up his presentation with some trendy cultural references. To the Greeks, poetry had deep significance. It was through poetry that their history, philosophies, and understanding of the divine were preserved. In this encounter, Paul builds his gospel case on the foundation of the Athenians' religious sculptures, sense of wonder and mystery, and words of their cherished poets.

While some mocked his presentation, others were interested in future dialogues. The Bible lists two individuals by name in this latter group: Damaris and Dionysius the Areopagite (Acts 17:34). Luke, the author of this narrative, assumed these two individuals were significant enough to his readers that he chose to mention them by name.

Dionysiou Areopagitou Street

Damaris is one of just a small number of women mentioned by name in the New Testament. As for Dionysius the Areopagite, if you visit Athens today and hike to the Acropolis, you can walk down Dionysiou Areopagitou Street. Paul tapped into the culture to engage with people, who in turn impacted their culture in ways that are still evident centuries later.

Paul's presentation was built on a firm propositional reality that was rational. Rather than argue with his listeners, he pinpointed the desires of their innermost being and then used the language of the heart to aim them toward Jesus.

A Satisfying Taste

In Acts 17, Paul provides an example of what it looks like to speak the language of the heart amid a culture dominated by pagan spirituality, aesthetics, narrative, and desire. There is one final component of a heart appeal, and that is the aim or purpose. What do we hope to accomplish by engaging our culture in this way?

A repeated metaphor in the Bible for an encounter with God through faith is "taste" (Ps. 34:8; Heb. 6:4–5; 1 Pet. 2:3). It is compelling because of the uniqueness of our sense of taste. Despite belonging to the "culinary arts," the sense of taste is rarely included in the high arts (there is no culinary wing at the Louvre, for example). When food *is* classified as an art, it is typically being used as raw material for a different artistic medium (like a chocolate sculpture). The reason for its exclusion from the high arts is that food cannot sufficiently communicate anything beyond its own essence.[‡]

---

‡ As the delightful Pixar movie *Ratatouille* captured, our sense of taste *can* evoke powerful memories. We taste a pie that reminds us of "how Momma used to make it" and are instantly transported back to our idyllic childhood years. But the pie itself is not communicating "the innocence of childhood." In fact, the ability of taste to ignite powerful memories is largely *because* food communicates itself so distinctly and singularly.

A culture driven by affections is
primed to receive the gospel.

Musical notes can be combined in a vast range of harmonies or melodies, and these can then be used to compose a song or symphony. Colors can be mixed to form entirely new hues, which can then be blended and used to create an endless range of images. But a strawberry can only ever taste like a strawberry. It may taste juicy and fresh or rotten and sour, but it remains a strawberry nonetheless.

A skilled chef may combine that strawberry with other ingredients to make a cake, but our tongues still taste strawberry, just in a new way. The cake cannot express themes or cultivate emotion the way music and visuals can transcend their essence into something greater.§ Therefore, when the biblical authors write of "tasting" the goodness of God, it is to know and experience God as He truly is.

As Christians, we have "tasted that the Lord is good" (1 Pet. 2:3). Jesus put it more graphically: "Whoever eats my flesh and drinks my blood remains in me, and I in them" (John 6:56). No wonder the early Christians were accused of cannibalism! The Great Commission is essentially Jesus calling His followers to make more disciples who come to know and experience Him in this way (Matt. 28:16–20).

---

§ Consider that we can hear and see beauty, but we can't "taste" beauty. Instead, we evaluate food as "good or bad," depending on how well (or poorly) it expresses its own expected essence. Unlike in music, where a minor chord can communicate "melancholy" or "sorrow," it may be difficult to convince someone that the taste of rotten fruit expresses anything other than a need to finally put those moldy bananas into the garbage can.

Ultimately, this is the goal of even the most head-centric approaches to apologetics. Rational and scientific arguments about God are not just about transplanting ideas from one brain into another. Rather, such tools are a way for Christians to nudge unbelievers closer to the banquet table to experience Christ for themselves.

As we know, reading a menu can spark interest, but smelling the first wafts from the kitchen can get us salivating. The Bible describes Christians as "the aroma of Christ" and the "fragrance" of life (2 Cor. 2:15–16 ESV). Christ offers to satisfy our hunger and quench our thirst (John 6:35). Once we have tasted this for ourselves, we can become like the aroma of fresh bread drawing people to the banquet table.

The mythologist Joseph Campbell is said to have mused, "Preachers err ... by trying 'to talk people into belief; better they reveal the radiance of their own discovery.'"[11] Only God can provide the feast, but we can diffuse the aroma of the banquet table into our culture.

Straight to the Heart

A culture driven by affections is primed to receive the gospel. Our world is starving for that which will finally satisfy their unquenchable spiritual hunger. As Christians with bellies full of abundance from God, we can help lead them there.

Throughout the remainder of this book, we will explore several ways our hearts draw us into deeper intimacy with God while also connecting to the pulse of our culture to help others come to experience that same faith. We hope these chapters will provide practical suggestions on how to speak the various dialects of the heart language.

At the same time, this book is not meant to be a handbook for cultural engagement or apologetics or a step-by-step manual for spiritual formation. Rather, we hope to inspire you to explore the depths of the human heart, both in how you relate to God in your own faith and in how you communicate the gospel to the world around you.

The realms through which we will journey are sometimes ambiguous and hard to quantify. What can make them daunting can also make them exciting. We all feel more comfortable with answers than with questions, but it is often the mystique itself that draws us in. The human heart is a fascinating and mysterious place. Let's journey there together.

Part 2

Speaking the Heart Language

Chapter 4

Story

Reading literature, more than informing us, forms us.
—Karen Swallow Prior

We have come from God ... and inevitably the
myths woven by us, though they contain error,
will also reflect a splintered fragment of the true
light, the eternal truth that is with God.
—J. R. R. Tolkien

The Day We Thought We'd Die

Growing up in Canada, our family would sometimes visit the famous West Edmonton Mall. One of its many attractions was an indoor amusement park and its renowned centerpiece: the Mindbender—at the time, the largest indoor roller coaster in the world. As we entered the park, the shrieks of terrified riders would echo down from the rafters, and we would crane our necks to behold the monster looming over us.

You may think we're exaggerating, but people had literally *died* riding it. Still, our thrill-loving father was quick to assure us, "I think that was a long time ago," and each year he invited us to face our fears and ride it with him. Brave warrior souls as we were, we would reply, "Absolutely, unequivocally, unwaveringly, without further question or debate: *No.*" This ritual continued year after year, the same question followed by the same answer.

Until one year, something changed. Our scheming father sprang a new tactic on us: he invited two of our best friends who he knew were daredevils. They took one look at the roller coaster stretching to the

Mindbender roller coaster

ceiling and *begged* to ride it. Peer pressure began to work its magic. Checkmate. We caved and agreed to do it. After all, we trusted our father and we (sort of) trusted our friends.

Tension built as we waited in the long, winding line for our turn. We were too terrified to breathe but too prideful to turn back. Second thoughts screamed in our heads as the restraining device was clicked firmly into place (at least we *hoped* it was firm!). As the car ascended higher and higher toward the heavens, we saw an incredible view of the entire amusement park—a final blessing before what we were sure was to be our messy end.

The coaster finally reached the top, pausing for just a moment, then plunged down the steep drop. Our high-pitched squeals were drowned out by the deafening roar of the ride as it raced into a triple-loop combination.

What an unforgettable thrill! Turns out, our father knew that if we would just trust him and face our fears, we would open ourselves up to an exciting new world of experiences. Since that day, we have conquered countless amusement parks, ridden even bigger rides, and have even gone bungee jumping into the Corinth Canal.

Not long after that initial ride, Mike had an opportunity to share the gospel with a young lady visiting our church. Her father was fiercely opposed to Christianity, and she was understandably nervous about committing her life to Jesus. As a youth without much evangelistic training or experience, Mike was unsure how to best explain faith to her. Then he remembered the fear, followed by the thrill, of that roller coaster. "Let me tell you a story about stepping out in faith ..."

He recounted the fear that keeps many people watching from the sidelines. We can hear people share their experiences and even watch others take action, but until we put our trust in our *heavenly* Father and take a step of faith ourselves, we'll never experience the thrill of a relationship with Jesus. The step of faith may terrify us, but it is the entryway into an unforgettable life that must be experienced firsthand.

Something about the story clicked in this young lady's heart that day. She wept as she prayed and made her own commitment of faith, trusting her heavenly Father's invitation to experience the thrill of eternal life that lay ahead.

A Storytelling People

Stories draw us in. From the ancient art adorning cave walls to present-day role-playing video games, humans have used stories to understand the world and our place within it. Narratives give form to abstract realities, allowing us to *feel* truth. A story becomes both the window through which we understand our own immediate experience and the framework to understand bigger truths about God and faith.

Stories are everywhere. There are obvious examples, such as books, movies, and sad country songs, but narrative permeates culture in many other forms as well. Advertisers weave persuasive tales, selling stories more than products.* Sports broadcasters heighten tension by spinning stories of human drama.† Politicians adopt amplified public personas and then frame their campaigns as inspiring narratives in which they are the heroes in a dire struggle against their villainous opponents for the soul of the nation.

At any given moment, countless narratives are washing over us, vying for our attention and shaping our lives. If we desire to be effective in engaging our Heart Culture, we must come to recognize the stories being told. Not only that, but we must also learn to contribute to the cultural canon. To speak the language of the heart is to function as storytellers.

Stories in a Heart Culture

We once heard a fascinating interview with one of the editors of the reality show *The Bachelorette*. She explained that her team is given *hundreds* of hours of raw footage, the vast majority of which is never seen by the public. The editor then has the power to choose which story to tell. Depending on what scenes she selects (or discards) and how she arranges them, she can dramatically develop different narratives, creating heroes and villains, emphasizing certain plots, and

---

* The perfume industry has historically been among the biggest spenders for commercial ads—more than $800 million a year—despite the fact that their product cannot actually be communicated through that medium (you can't smell through a TV screen). This is because they aren't selling scents as much as the stories attached to them.

† Mike's wife watches the Olympics almost exclusively for the inspiring real-life stories.

even manufacturing false drama. While she cannot change the raw material—the "reality" component—she nevertheless has the power to shape it into whatever story she and the studio executives decide to tell.

It's possible to conclude that the role of stories in our culture is limited to fabricating fiction based on selected material. Conspiracy theories catch fire when desirable narratives overpower the rational objections of the mind. Hollywood is increasingly criticized for using stories to disseminate harmful ideologies, especially to children.

News outlets are rightly accused of brokering narratives rather than unbiased facts; the same event can sound nearly unrecognizable depending on what channel or website you visit. The headline usually tells you what angle the writers are coming from ("Controversial Author Sparks Protests" as opposed to "Popular Speaker Draws Large Crowd"). As a result, Christians may develop an attitude of mistrust toward stories as a reliable vehicle for expressing truth.

Yet, while some storytellers do indeed wield stories for destructive and misleading purposes, a well-told narrative can also be imbued with edifying, clarifying, and redemptive power.

Stories *can* be escapist, transporting us into realms of fantasy, but they are also one of the most effective ways to understand and communicate our experiences. In fact, to a degree, we cannot fully understand our circumstances *without* a narrative framework.

In 1976, Christian philosopher James Sire wrote a classic book on worldviews called *The Universe Next Door*. The concepts were originally conceived amid a Head Culture, but in the subsequent editions, the emergence of a Heart Culture shifted the discussion. In the preface of a later edition, he explains that an increased understanding of the "biblical notion of the heart" led him to revise his earlier definitions and concepts in several ways, including giving more emphasis to "pretheoretical roots" of the intellect, and by expanding the way that worldview is expressed through "the notion of story."[1]

Sire's original scholarship set the standard for how many later Christians came to understand "worldview formation" as an intellectual pursuit. However, he ultimately realized that a worldview is formed predominantly in the heart, and a key element to that is the power of story.

Perhaps this is why so much of the Bible appears in narrative form and why Jesus' primary method of communicating the kingdom of God was through parables. That stories can be used to harmful ends does not preclude Christians from using them effectively for spiritual edification.

Stories have always been important, but within a Heart Culture that puts heightened value on narrative, they present a unique opportunity to connect with others. We can speak this dialect of the heart language by leveraging three key story types: (1) the stories we live, (2) the stories we tell, and (3) the stories others tell.

Three Story Types
Type 1: The Stories We Live

Life as a Story

Mythologist Joseph Campbell popularized the theory of *the hero's journey*, the classic universal story structure that has tremendously influenced Hollywood (*Star Wars* creator George Lucas referred to Campbell as "my Yoda").[2] To Campbell, the hero's journey—or "monomyth"—was universal because it could be detected in the myths of every human culture in history and also because it embodied spiritual truths. It was not just a story structure for the stories we tell. It was a reflection of the stories we live.

Today's psychologists have affirmed this. We not only find guidance *from* stories, but at a fundamental level we understand our own lives in terms of an unfolding story This is evident in the language we use: "I'm closing the book on that relationship" or "I'm ready to begin the next chapter of my life." Susan Cain writes:

> At the Foley Center for the Study of Lives at Northwestern University, [Dan] McAdams studies the stories that people tell about themselves. We all write our life stories as if we were novelists, McAdams believes, with beginnings, conflicts, turning points, and endings. And the way we characterize our past setbacks profoundly influences how satisfied we are with our current lives.[3]

Psychologist Jonathan Haidt notes the concept of "posttraumatic growth," in which those who come to make sense of traumatic events by seeing them as part of their life stories and writing them out into meaningful narratives experience better physical health up to a year later as compared to those who cannot see their suffering within this context.[4]

Similarly, psychologist Daniel Kahneman describes people as having an "experiencing self" and a "remembering self." We experience the world in real time, but those experiences quickly become memories of the past. In many ways, we *are* our remembering selves, because we weave our memories into a coherent narrative to understand past events.[5]

This is likely our subconscious motivation when we spend time capturing the perfect Instagram picture rather than being fully engaged in the moment as it's happening. We know the experience itself is brief, but we can relive the *memory* of it countless times through the monument of our social media post.

Invitation into a Greater Story

If it's true that people understand their lives as part of an unfolding story, then this can inform how we share the gospel with others. Rather than presenting an intellectual position to adopt, we can invite people into an unfolding story. Better yet, we can help them understand that they already are part of that narrative, whether they recognize it or not.

The classic hymn "Victory in Jesus" begins with the refrain "I heard an old, old story." It is a helpful reminder that Scripture is not just isolated texts or concepts but presents us with a unified narrative. This does not mean that every human author contributing to the Bible knew he was adding a chapter to a greater work. Rather, the larger whole takes form as the individual pieces come together, like the ingredients of a recipe. Contributions from different writers in various genres across vast stretches of history find their unity and fulfillment in the person of Jesus (Luke 24:27).

"In the beginning" (Gen. 1:1) is perhaps the inspiration of the classic "Once upon a time." With those words, God set the stage for the tale of how He saved humanity from sin and death. This epic narrative spans thousands of years and has all the elements of the best stories:

thrilling battles, underdog victories, romance, betrayal, journeys, trag-
edy, comedy, supernatural encounters—even dragons (Rev. 12:3)! The
theme of creation, fall, and redemption has inspired countless imita-
tions, interpretations, and reimaginings.

C. S. Lewis referred to the gospel as "the true myth," since it possessed the same exciting features as the pagan mythology he loved but
with the staggering difference that it actually happened.[6]

We may be tempted to reduce the gospel to a formula ("The
ABC's of Becoming a Christian" or "The Roman Road") that can be
used as an evangelist's elevator pitch. Such efficiency has advantages.
It allows us to communicate the gospel quickly. But are we communicating it *effectively*? How much story fits into one minute, and
what understanding is achieved without the needed context? Such
a presentation usually doesn't carry as much weight within a Heart
Culture. That's because the gospel is not a formula for a Christian or
a recipe for a saint; it's a story we participate in. Perhaps what makes a
gospel presentation attractive is not its efficient brevity but its aston-
ishing cosmic scope, and how we—so small in the grand scheme of
things—are part of it.

When Jesus spoke of the kingdom of God, He frequently alluded
to the Old Testament prophets, or even to creation itself. His invitation
to "Come, follow Me" was not drawing followers into a new start-up
religion like a first-century entrepreneur. It was an opportunity to join
in a story that God had been unfolding for a *long* time. People in a
Heart Culture already understand their lives as a progressing story. As
we present our faith, we can do so by inviting them to participate in a
bigger story—the true myth—that continues to unfold.

Shaping the Narrative

It's not uncommon to hear celebrity publicists speak about "controlling the narrative" after their client makes a social *faux pas*. There is the truth of a situation, and then there is how people perceive that truth, and both are important. The Bible urges Christians to abstain from "all *appearance* of evil" (1 Thess. 5:22 KJV). We know that Christians should avoid evil, and yet the perception of evil—even if false—can be just as damaging to our witness.

We typically think of cultural engagement in terms of individual encounters, but those encounters inevitably take place within a larger narrative. For example, those who "deconstruct" their childhood faith often speak in broader terms than just the local congregation that was home to their negative experiences. Their disillusionment toward religion was not an isolated event but part of a perception of the church on a larger scale (e.g., "*The church* isn't a safe place for doubts," or "*The church* isn't welcoming").

In a Heart Culture, we should be intentional about how our words and actions shape the wider narrative about Christianity. This does not mean presenting a *false* story. Tragically, some churches have attempted to save face by covering up immoral and abusive behavior, and have contributed to a narrative of a religion more concerned with outward appearances than protecting the vulnerable.

Shaping the narrative is not always a manipulative PR spin. It may also mean being conscious of the story the world is actually perceiving and how that might be different from what we think it is. We practice this intuitively when we clarify, "Our church is *not* like …" or when we feel we owe further explanation for terms like *evangelical*. Our cultural encounters with people do not occur in a vacuum. They take place within a noisy and confusing sea of prior experiences and narratives that—fairly or unfairly—influence how our actions and message are received.

How we express our faith matters. We might feel virtuous for taking a bold stand on social media and "just speaking the truth," and yet we may fail to see that what we actually did was reinforce the cultural narrative that Christians are graceless and self-righteous. These wider effects on our reputation may be a net cultural loss in the long run.

Stories get planted deep within us, and once a narrative takes root—true or false—it is hard to remove. If a Heart Culture makes sense of the world through narratives, then Christians have a vested interest in ensuring that our words and actions contribute to a narrative that does not misrepresent Jesus.

Type 2: The Stories We Tell

We All Have Stories to Tell

In the Old Testament, the Hebrew people were commanded to retell the stories of God's activity as part of their history (see Ex. 12:25-27; Josh. 4:19–24; Ps. 145:4). They had a responsibility to pass this knowledge on to the next generation, lest it disappear from their collective memory.

In a Head Culture, the personal testimony and experiences of Christians can become targets of ridicule from unbelievers as listeners demand more objective evidence for our claims. In contrast, a Heart Culture elevates subjectivity to a position of authority where my "lived experience" leads to "my truth." This presents a great opportunity. A governing principle of a Heart Culture is that people should openly accept the stories that others tell about themselves. Why not add our own to the mix?

In the New Testament, Paul gives his personal testimony five times. This self-proclaimed "chief of sinners" had a good story to tell, and he did so often. If you are a Christian, you have one too, and everyone loves a good redemption arc. And a good sequel! What has God done in your life *since* your conversion?

Our mother jokes about the fear she once had whenever she saw our grandfather because she knew he was always going to ask, "What has God been doing in your life lately?" She recalls how she'd needed to prepare ahead of time with our father, asking him in a panic, "Quick, Henry is coming over—what has God been doing in my life?"‡

We do people a disservice if we act as though our salvation testimony is the *end* of our stories. It might be more appropriately seen as the middle. There were events that led up to that moment, and experiences that have continued after.

What has God done in your life *this past week*? If your answer is "nothing," think about it a little harder. It may be that we have never learned to recognize God's activity around us. Perhaps we are not stepping out in faith to places where such stories are made. We all want to experience miracles, but we are not sure we want to be in situations where miracles are *needed*! The truth is that everyone loves to hear a good story, and God is in the business of directing some incredible ones.

An elderly man in Mike's church has countless "God stories." He has traveled around the world and lived a full life, experiencing

---

‡ For the record, our mom has *lots* of great stories of God working in her life. She just couldn't remember well under pressure!

God's miraculous power on many occasions. One time, a woman asked him why he seemed to have so many of these stories while she had so few. He offered this possible explanation: "Whenever God does something in my life, I tell *everybody* about it. Might it be that because I am quick to share these stories with others, God sees fit to give me more?"

Story Structures

What if we took an even broader view of narrative? What if we saw story not just as individual tales we tell but as a universally relatable, overarching structure that we utilize in our teaching, sermons, Bible studies, and small-group discussions?

Bible teachers sometimes scratch the narrative itch of their listeners by including a story or two in their delivery. Eugene L. Lowry takes this further and suggests that the teaching itself can follow the structure of a story by following a plot: start with a felt tension that people can identify with and then take people on a journey (anchored in the biblical text) to find resolution in the gospel.[7] We know the solution will be "Jesus," but we don't know how we will end up there. This provides the tension, drawing people in as participants rather than just as observers.[8]

Daniel had a college professor who once bemoaned the fact that students would sit through a two-hour movie yet struggle to stay engaged for a thirty-minute class, despite the latter being more mentally beneficial. What he failed to see was that it was not (just) about apathetic students but about two vastly different communication structures. Stories offer a sense of movement and discovery that traditional teaching rarely does. If our sermons and lessons feel more like lectures than stories, we should not be surprised when they are easily ignored or forgotten by a Heart Culture.

Like the "call to adventure" phase in the hero's journey, your sermons or Bible studies can follow an unfolding plot that invites your listeners on a journey of discovery *with* you. Rather than give them the answer up front ("Here's what Paul said about discipleship ..."), begin with a relevant question resulting from living in a fallen world ("Is there anything about your character you wish you could change? Why are we never satisfied with who we are?"). Then set out on your quest for an answer to that felt need.

Along the way, you'll describe setbacks in the form of false solutions ("The world says _____, but here's why that won't completely fix the problem ..."). Your protagonist will also come in contact with "allies" and "mentors" (quotes, illustrations, Scriptures, etc.—"Psychologists tell us that we are habit-forming creatures, often unintentionally ...").

Eventually, you will arrive at a place where all hope seems lost ("At our core, we long to be more than who we are, but we don't know how to change ..."). The hero must die to his self-sufficiency and experience a rebirth. This is the point in the story where Jesus appears on the horizon like Gandalf in *The Two Towers* to lift the listeners to victory, leaving them changed and ready to go forth and invest their lives in others ("In 1 Timothy 4:6–10, Paul challenged Timothy to form *new* habits: '*Train* yourself for godliness.' However, this is only possible 'because we have our hope set on the living God ...'").

In a Heart Culture, we can leverage the power of stories not just by telling them but also by harnessing the elements—tension, struggle, discovery, obstacle, and victory—that captivate our imaginations.

Type 3: The Stories Others Tell

Imaginary Influencers

We try to resist impulse buying, but at one grocery store checkout a particular magazine title proved irresistible to Daniel: *TIME* magazine's "The 100 Most Influential People Who Never Lived." Daniel threw it on the conveyor belt (along with some Tic-Tacs, a chocolate bar, and an electronic plug-in converter he didn't need). Part of the magazine edition's introduction said this:

> Fictional characters are all around us, the secret sharers of our hopes and fears, the companions of our childhood, the signposts that mark the waystations in our lives.... Fiction offers a wonderful way for the creators among us to distill the essence of basic human traits into pure form, then bring them to memorable life in the guise of an outsized exemplar.[9]

Fiction impacts us because it is like a mirror that allows us to see our own humanity more clearly. The imaginary characters might appear larger than life, but their journeys—and the lessons they learn along the way—are vehicles for storytellers to explore the relatable experiences of everyday life. Novelist F. Scott Fitzgerald wrote that in stories, "You discover that your longings are universal longings, that you're not lonely and isolated from anyone. You belong."[10] The best stories are those that capture our human nature and spirit.

So far, we have suggested that we should recognize our lives as an unfolding story and should strive to be effective storytellers ourselves.

Additionally, in a culture permeated by stories, sometimes we need only use what is already available to us. If a heart-centric approach to cultural engagement is one that begins with listening rather than talking, then a fruitful starting point is to turn to the stories already being told all around us.

Signposts and Signals

J. R. R. Tolkien believed that all the stories we tell "reflect a splintered fragment of the true light."[11] Some storytellers build sandcastles to glorify God, and others erect structures that blaspheme God, but both are created from the sand of God's sandbox. All storytellers are created in the image of God and use their narratives to explore our existence in a world He created.

As a result, most stories provide signposts that point back to God in some way. James Sire calls these "signals of transcendence."[12]§ They are moments when our stories begin probing the bigger questions of God's story.

Sometimes a story wrestles with spiritual questions directly (as in Shūsaku Endō's *Silence*), while in other stories God is conspicuous by His absence (e.g., the John Wick franchise). A story can be told to glorify God (Lewis's Chronicles of Narnia) or to mock Him (Philip Pullman's *His Dark Materials*). Some stories are deeply religious, while others—such as a sitcom—may focus on the mundane experiences of life in a seemingly nonreligious world.

---

§ Sire borrows the term from sociologist Peter Berger's book, *A Rumor of Angels*, and applies the concept to literature.

All of these stories can be signposts and signals. In a Heart Culture, we can discover what questions matter most to people by looking at the stories they tell and the stories they are drawn to.

During his time as a pastor to young adults, Mike began every message with a movie clip. The intention was for it to be more than just a fun icebreaker; it was also a way to demonstrate that the gospel has satisfying answers to the types of questions, doubts, and desires our culture is exploring. One night, an individual came up to him and half-jokingly declared, "I can't watch any movie now without seeing the worldview behind it!"

> A Heart Culture that has elevated personal narrative to a place of moral authority is primed to understand their lives as part of God's bigger story.

Stories can be an amazing gateway to spiritual conversations if we approach them with thoughtful openness. A Heart Culture desires a faith that connects to the world they live in. We can demonstrate how the same Jesus we proclaim from the pulpit also intersects with the stories they love and are already immersed in every day.

Conclusion

Stories are all around us. We shape the narratives of our culture, even as they shape us. From books we read, movies we watch, news we hear, social media posts we scroll through, billboards we drive by, and beyond, we can see that the Heart Culture is a world of discordant stories vying for our heart's attention.

There's an old proverb that goes: "Tell me the facts, and I'll learn. Tell me the truth, and I'll believe. But tell me a story, and it will live in my heart forever." Stories have power to penetrate the heart and shape us from the inside out. In a culture of competing narratives, the only question is which stories will form the metanarrative that directs our lives.

Stories are a powerful part of our spiritual heritage. We are story-telling people, created in the image of a God who continually reveals Himself to us through narrative. We have an incredible opportunity to speak new stories into our culture, even as we help them rediscover "the greatest story ever told."

A Heart Culture that has elevated personal narrative to a place of moral authority is primed to understand their lives as part of God's bigger story. In a narrative-driven Heart Culture, we all have a story to share. What stories will you tell?

Chapter 5

Beauty

*Never lose an opportunity of seeing anything that
is beautiful. Beauty is God's handwriting.*

—Charles Kingsley

There is no defense against beauty.... Beauty is irresistible.

—Peter Kreeft

Behold the Monkey!

In 2012, an alleged crime took a twist that nobody saw coming—and earned a place in cultural infamy. Local authorities in Borja, Spain, were called to investigate an act of vandalism to a painting displayed in the sanctuary of Mercy Church. A 1930s fresco painting called *Ecce Homo* ("Behold the Man"), depicting Jesus with a crown of thorns, had been defaced in a monstrous way. Had the deed been motivated by antagonism toward the church? Was it a nefarious act of blasphemy? The answer turned out to be something much different.

The act was not vandalism at all. It was a *restoration*, the handiwork of an eighty-one-year-old amateur artist named Cecilia Giménez. She was troubled by the deteriorated condition of the original painting and took it upon herself to restore it. Unfortunately, things didn't go as planned. Rather than channeling the sublime beauty of the suffering Savior, the "restored" Jesus had a demented appearance that one journalist described as a "crayon sketch of a very hairy monkey in an ill-fitting tunic."[1] The botched restoration attempt quickly went viral on the internet, where it was dubbed *Ecce Mono* ("Behold the Monkey").

Ecce Homo: original, damaged, and "restored"

Alberto Paredes / Alamy Stock Photo

You may be familiar with that part of the story, but you may not know that the tale didn't end there. The legend of *Ecce Mono* continued to grow and change over time. As a result of its newfound fame, thousands of tourists flocked to the church, with the admission fees going to support the church's mission and home for the elderly. An Interpretation Center and museum was eventually established in dedication to the artwork. Or, more specifically, to the story of its creation: the endearing tale of an elderly woman who gave her all in an act of worship to her Lord.

A decade later, a tribute in the *New York Post* declared, "More than the 10th anniversary of the artistic snafu, it also marks the event's progression from a worldwide embarrassment, to an economic saving grace, to a lesson in forgiveness and support."[2]

Somehow, one of the world's ugliest works of art became the catalyst for something heartwarming and—dare we say—*beautiful*.

Inexplicable Beauty

Beauty is a notoriously tricky concept. When Daniel gives talks on aesthetics, he sometimes displays the failed *Ecce Homo* restoration alongside a quaint landscape painting. Without context, he asks the audience which picture is more beautiful (i.e., which they would rather hang in their homes). As expected, the charming landscape always

Painting by aspiring young German artist

wins. Then he provides the backstory of the two artists and reveals that the picturesque landscape was painted by an aspiring young German artist by the name of Adolf Hitler. At that point, many in the room inevitably wish to change their vote.

We have been conditioned to think of beauty primarily as a matter of attractive outward appearances, but there is more to it than that. There is a mystical element that can draw us to an artistic atrocity like the restored *Ecce Homo* rather than a work by an evil dictator, no matter how accomplished the form or technique. This is because beauty is not restricted to just our visual or auditory senses. It is something deeper and ethereal, a gift imperfectly captured as an echo of a more transcendent reality. The beauty of the physical and material world is like a melody that rings in our minds, a memory of a sublime symphony we once heard and yearn to hear again.

Beauty is a crucial ingredient to all human flourishing, but it is not just a head-in-the-clouds topic discussed by snobby artists and ivory-tower aestheticians. It is also a vital aspect of the Christian faith and our cultural engagement.

As we have seen, a Heart Culture's rejection of Christianity is not primarily because of the church's rational failings but due to a lost *attraction* to faith. Without beauty, graceless fundamentalism and self-righteous judgmentalism have a tendency to fill the gaps in the Christian message, repelling the culture rather than drawing it in. Christianity without beauty is a movie without a soundtrack. It confronts minds but leaves hearts unstirred.

We must rediscover the importance of beauty, not as something extra sprinkled into life, but as a foundational value grounded in God's divine nature. Our heads may try to rationalize away beauty as trivial, but our souls yearn for it, because we yearn for God—the source of beauty. To speak the language of the heart is ultimately to open ourselves to the gift of beauty and to let others know where this priceless treasure can be found.

Theology of Beauty

A fascinating quirk of history is how Charles Darwin lost his appreciation for beauty. He was initially captivated by it, famously concluding *On the Origin of Species* with a poetic celebration of "endless forms most beautiful"[3] and using the words "beauty" and "beautiful" 280 times in *Descent of Man*.[4] But in journals written near the end of his life, he confessed that he had lost a taste for beauty and aesthetics. He found himself unable to enjoy a symphony and so bored by great works of literature like Shakespeare that he felt nauseated. He lamented:

> My mind seems to have become a kind of machine....
> If I had to live my life again, I would have made a rule
> to read some poetry and listen to some music at least

once every week; for perhaps the parts of my brain
now atrophied could thus have been kept active
through use.[5]

Darwin perceived beauty in the world but was unable to reconcile
that reality with his naturalistic worldview. By knocking down the
divine foundation for creation, he also removed the only firm cornerstone from which an understanding of beauty can be constructed.
Beauty pointed his heart in directions that the naturalistic worldview
in his head was unwilling to travel.

The nineteenth-century French novelist Gustave Flaubert
declared, "The time for beauty is over. Mankind may return to it, but
it has no use for it at present. The more Art develops, the more scientific it will be."[6] Nancy Pearcey rightly observes, "The public has a
hard time understanding why many modern artists have rejected the
ideal of beauty. But it is understandable when we realize that it was a
consequence of a ruthless naturalistic worldview."[7]

For beauty to play a meaningful role in our lives and in how we
interact with the wider culture, we must first return beauty to its right-
ful place as a property that radiates from God's being and is reflected
in His ways. Peter Kreeft writes: "Beauty is to God what sunlight is
to the sun. Beauty is God's *shining*. It acts on us, not we on it. We can
choose only to receive it or to not receive it, but we cannot turn it on
or off."[8]

The influential art critic Arthur C. Danto observed: "Beauty is
the only one of the aesthetic qualities that is also a value, like truth and
goodness. It is not simply among the values we live by, but one of the
values that defines what a fully human life means."[9]

> Christianity without beauty is a movie
> without a soundtrack. It confronts
> minds but leaves hearts unstirred.

Danto is appealing to a classical philosophical concept called the *transcendentals*, or as it's more commonly known, "The good, the true, and the beautiful" (a phrase that one of our seminary professors liked to claim as the title of his autobiography!). The roots of the concept are Greek, but it has frequently been adapted and applied to Christian theology by thinkers such as Thomas Aquinas and Augustine.

The concept is theologically rich and complex, pointing to three properties of God, who is a being of truth, goodness, and beauty. God is both the source of these values and the perfect realization of them. Just as God becomes the absolute standard by which we measure and define truth or morality, so too is He the standard for beauty.

From here, we can establish three important characteristics of beauty.

1. Beauty Is Objective

As the popular saying goes, "Beauty is in the eye of the beholder." While Christians have fought in the cultural trenches to preserve truth and goodness as absolutes, we have largely exiled beauty to the island of relativism. After all, if we cannot all agree on what is beautiful, then it must be a subjective reality, right?

Not exactly. The objectivity of something is never dependent on universal consensus or a majority vote. That people can debate truth

claims ("Is 2 + 2 *really* 4?") does not mean that truth is subjective—
only that some perceive the truth more clearly than others. If beauty
derives from God, then it is objectively beautiful. If not all people can
recognize this beauty, then the problem is in our inability to perceive
it. The apostle Paul wrote that God's eternal nature and divine power
is made plain to us through creation, even if many in their wickedness
fail to accept it (Rom. 1:18–20).

Much of the subjective disagreement about beauty is a matter
of aesthetic tastes rather than a statement on beauty itself. We may
prefer one artistic style over another or be attracted to certain physical
characteristics more than others, but this points to our own personal
preferences. If someone were to deny the beauty of a mother's love for
a newborn baby, for example, and attempt to frame it as something
grotesque, we would not affirm the value of their subjective opinion.
We would lament the scales on their eyes that prevent them from perceiving the objective beauty before them.

A father who tells his young daughter "Beauty is in the eye
of the beholder" is inadvertently giving the power to the eyes of
male beholders: "You are beautiful if a man thinks you are."* A
Christian understanding of beauty is far more satisfying than that.
The husband who finds his wife "more beautiful every day" is not
increasing his bride's beauty; he is merely discovering it more fully
by diving deeper into its existing depths—both in the physical and
the immaterial.

---

* In the classic role-playing game Dungeons and Dragons, a "Beholder" is a grotesque monster, a
globular shape with protruding eyes. There is something fitting about the depiction in relation
to this classic mantra.

2. Beauty Is the Fragrance of Truth and Goodness

The English poet John Keats wrote, "Beauty is truth, truth beauty,—that is all / Ye know on earth, and all ye need to know."[10] While some beauty belongs to the visual and auditory realms, there is another dimension of beauty that reveals itself as an outpouring of God's goodness and truth. Philosopher Dietrich von Hildebrand calls this beauty the "fragrance" of virtue.[11]

Beauty is the aroma that derives from the truth and goodness that reflect God's character and design. The author of Ecclesiastes explores this framework for beauty: "He has made everything beautiful in its time" (Eccl. 3:11a). We encounter biblical beauty when things function as God intended—in that which is true and good.

We innately recognize this whenever an adoring mother declares "It's beautiful!" as her young child presents her with his latest artistic creation—a technical abomination of misunderstood proportions and clashing colors. There *is* something beautiful embedded in that drawing, even if an artist would be unlikely to include it in her portfolio for admission to art school. There is something fitting about a young child offering his best work as a demonstration of love to his parents.

The same might be said about the wrinkles in an elderly grandmother's face after a lifetime of laughter, in contrast to the narcissistic vanity espoused through cosmetics magazines. The same fruit in Eden that was "pleasing to the eye" (Gen. 3:6) became an ugly symbol of sin and shame—the "forbidden fruit"—when experienced outside of God's design. The same Roman cross that was a grotesque instrument of death became a beautiful symbol of victory after Christ's resurrection. There is beauty in that which operates in harmony with God's intentions.

3. Beauty Is Transcendent

Following the statement that God made everything beautiful in its time, the author of Ecclesiastes adds, "He has also set eternity in the hearts of men, yet they cannot fathom the work that God has done from beginning to end" (3:11b BSB). Embedded in beauty is something transcendent and beyond our material world.

Perhaps this is why God's design for both the tabernacle and temple included nonfunctional objects intended for beauty. Beauty stirs our hearts toward its source. Hildebrand writes, "It contains a summons ... [and] it awakens awe in us; it elevates us above that which is base; it fills our hearts with a longing for the eternal beauty of God."[12] The experience of beauty activates the God-placed eternity in our hearts and nudges us toward the divine.

Terrible and Irresistible

Remember the H. G. Wells short book *The Country of the Blind* from a previous chapter? The story ends with a stimulating dialogue. Nunez has escaped the rockslide with his betrothed, Medina-saroté, but she resists medical treatment that could cure her blindness. Her reason is haunting:

> "The loveliness of your world is a complicated and
> fearful loveliness and mine is simple and near." [...]
> "But the beauty!" [...]
> "It may be beautiful," said Medina-saroté, "but it
> must be very terrible to *see*."[13]

Beauty demands something of us. It makes us keenly aware of our own smallness and declares the uncomfortable truth that there is more to reality than we may wish to accept. C. S. Lewis captured this truth in the Pevensie children's initial description of Aslan, the great lion of Narnia, as "good and terrible at the same time."[14]

This demanding quality is perhaps why the modernization and secularization of Western culture has seen a continual assault on beauty. The Modernist artists in the late nineteenth and early twentieth centuries largely expunged beauty from its pedestal as a pursuit of art. They did this both by mocking it and by redefining it as something subjective and trivial. But beauty cannot be held at bay for long. The dam is breaking, and a Heart Culture is rediscovering its power. Christians have an opportunity to demonstrate how God ultimately satisfies this yearning.

Beauty is not something that is *used*. Beauty is something that *is*. It is discovered rather than wielded. At the same time, that does not mean beauty has no practical role in the Christian life or mission. Philosopher Peter Kreeft writes:

> Beauty is also the most powerfully appealing, for we can easily defend ourselves against truth and against goodness—by rationalization, by ignoring, or by simple, stubborn, selfish pig-headedness. But there is no defense against beauty. Truth humbly knocks at your door with credentials—arguments—in its hand. Goodness makes demands but waits outside

your door for you to freely open to it. But beauty
seeps under all your doors and walls like water.
Unlike truth and goodness, beauty is irresistible.[15]

We all perceive beauty intuitively. We know whether we like a work of art or not before we can provide rational explanations for those feelings. That's why it is difficult—if not impossible—to convince someone that something is *not* beautiful once beauty stirs the heart. Beauty captures our souls without warning. Hildebrand wrote that as we behold beauty, "Our heart is filled with a desire for loftier regions about which this beauty speaks, and it looks upward with longing."[16]

There are at least three areas where beauty is relevant to the church as we seek to engage a Heart Culture.

1. Beauty in Creation

The Bible is clear that the majesty of creation points to the existence of its Creator and also reveals some of His qualities (Rom. 1:20; Ps. 19:1–4). To return to our earlier metaphor of the cinematic experience, if Scripture is the narrative structure, then nature adds an aesthetic dimension to deepen that knowledge. In reading Genesis, we encounter the truth of creation. When we stand outside, gazing at a cresting sunrise, we *feel* it.

It is likely no coincidence that the slide from religion to atheism parallels the increase of industrialization. The more people retreat from God's creation, the more they lose a sense of the divine. Our sprawling concrete jungles and immaterial digital universes seem an insurmountable distance from the lush garden of Eden.

That is not to say that beauty is absent from cities. After all, God's new creation will not be a restored garden of Eden but a new *Jerusalem*—a perfect union of natural and urban beauty (Rev. 21–22). There is a sublime beauty in the New York City skyline just as there is in a California redwood forest. But the beauty is of a different sort. Such beauty is "sub-creation" (to borrow Tolkien's terminology).[17] Manmade rather than God-made. The danger of industrialization is that it could sever the union between God's creation and our sub-creation in a way that erases God's beautiful handiwork, leaving us surrounded by our own creations.

James Cameron's *Avatar* films are among the most successful movies ever made. There are many reasons for their unprecedented success, but one of the draws is the lush fictional planet of Pandora. In fact, so potent was that beauty that following the initial film's release there developed a phenomenon called "post-*Avatar* depression."[18] After the immersive beauty of the film, viewers would leave the theater and return to lives that seemed bereft of splendor. Their hearts had been awakened with a desire for beauty, leaving the industrialized world seeming bland.

Cultivating Creation

To deepen our sense of the divine and to reach a Heart Culture, Christians can benefit from the beauty of creation in several ways.

Christians have a vested interest in cultivating the beauty of God's creation. This is humanity's first God-given task (Gen. 2:15), and it remains as important as ever. If the beauty of creation points toward God, then Christians should foster beauty in whatever community God has placed them in.

During the COVID-19 pandemic, Mike began a new hobby: gardening. Officially resigning himself to the class of "not being cool anymore," he decided to make use of the nine raised garden boxes that came with his newly purchased home. What a joy! Connecting back to our garden beginnings is often spiritually therapeutic. The dirt under our fingernails replaces the dirt in our hearts collected from hours of social media scrolling.

Does the world look to the church and see us cultivating and enjoying the beauty of creation? Have we been intentional in how we have taken care of the natural beauty *outside* our church doors? This simple act may prepare hearts for worship before people ever enter our worship center. Have we allowed a love of nature to be seen only as an environmentalist or "tree-hugger" pursuit, or are we still brought to awe and worship when we participate in God's creation?

Rethinking the Context of Our Cultural Encounters

The places to engage the Head Culture were lecture halls or debate stages. But these may not be the most fruitful settings to engage a Heart Culture with conversations about the divine. Even the ever-popular backdrop of a coffee shop may foster more of a head appeal than a heart appeal, being surrounded by manmade structures in a consumer-based institution.

To awaken people's spiritual eyes to the majesty of God, we can begin by focusing their physical eyes on the grandeur of His creation. The environment of worship matters. It works on the level of our subconscious, shaping how we think and feel about our experience. We may teach people about the glory of God, but if we do so from within the confines of the four beige walls of a classroom, that message will be competing against a barrage of contrary messages speaking to their hearts.

One of the most powerful baptisms Mike participated in was baptizing a young man in the Pacific Ocean off the coast of Canada. The subzero temperatures certainly made it memorable! The backdrop of sky, sea, and mountains stirred people's hearts and fostered a special spiritual experience. This is why some churches are establishing prayer gardens on their property. It's an attempt to fuse the beauty of the natural world with the place of worship.

The magnificence of a mountain range, the vastness of the sky, or the intricate details of a flower often invoke feelings of *awe*. In our current Heart Culture, an appreciation for the beauty of nature is associated more with New Age spiritualities than the Christian faith. These spiritual seekers have tapped into something powerful, even if their theology is misguided. They have heard the sublime soundtrack but have not yet witnessed the movie or grasped the narrative that places that music in its proper context. What if Christians rediscovered the power found in God's creation and helped people direct their awe a little higher?

The prominent scientist Francis Collins gives an account of his gradual conversion to Christianity. As a scientist and leader of the Human Genome Project, Collins was comfortably placed within a Head Culture. In fact, his own book of apologetics is titled *The Language of God: A Scientist Presents Evidence for Belief.* His logical brain grappled with the truth claims of Christianity, but it was actually *beauty* that finally brought him to a place of belief. He specifically mentions the wonder of looking through his first telescope and the emotion of hearing Beethoven's Third Symphony.[19]

The final leap of faith came while hiking in the Cascade Mountains of Washington and happening upon an enormous frozen waterfall. The beauty of this moment led him to kneel in the dewy grass and embrace belief in Jesus as Lord.[20] In his head, Collins possessed important contextual information to make sense of his experiences and point him specifically to Jesus, but it was his heart that moved him to act upon it.

2. Beauty in Created Things

Beauty can also be embedded in our own creations. One of the most ignored contexts for beauty is in our churches. According to the author of Hebrews, the tabernacle served as "a copy and shadow of what is in heaven" (Heb. 8:5). In a mysterious way, that which we create on earth below can echo what is above. As we have already seen, in that copy and shadow of heaven was artistic excellence, extravagant splendor, and beauty.

Largely as a result of the perceived excesses of the historical church, many Protestant churches today imagine God as the ultimate minimalist. The manner in which we design and decorate (or *don't* decorate) our churches says much. Yet, in the only record we have of God's own architectural preferences, He seems to demonstrate a penchant for the extravagant.

Perhaps our resistance to this idea is why many of us implicitly share in Judas's dismay at Mary pouring out a bottle of priceless perfume on Jesus' feet as a sign of worship, instead of using it for more "practical" concerns (John 12:1–8).

Jesus does not indicate that *all* resources should be recklessly poured out in a single display of extravagant faith like Mary's. Nor does God mandate that *all* places of worship be equally as grand as the tabernacle.

The early Christian church met for worship mostly in first-century homes (not exactly the extravagant Sagrada Familia in Barcelona). The tabernacle and the temple represented special moments in history and in the relationship between God and His chosen people. But at the onset of that important relationship, God took an active role in how He was represented and what His dwellings indicated about Him.

The old cathedrals were a purposeful attempt to capture beauty. Their floorplans were often laid out like a cross, with the central point containing the sacraments. As you entered the doors, you would begin in darkness lit only by the sunrays reflecting through the stained-glass windows depicting faithful saints of old. As you approached the sanctuary, your eyes would be drawn upward

Interior of Worcester Cathedral, in Worcester, Worcestershire, England, UK

toward the roof of the dome, the highest and most brightly lit part of the design, which was typically adorned with majestic artwork of the heavens. From the moment you entered, you were engaged in an inter-active role-play of the Christian life, with the design elements elevating your worship to the Lord.

In contrast, most church design today is driven by pragmatism rather than beauty. When aesthetic elements are used—lights and stage design—it is typically to draw our attention to the people on stage rather than to lift people's eyes toward heaven.

If the objective is to gather a crowd and appeal primarily to their head, then the location is irrelevant so long as the correct information is transferred. Perhaps this is why many churches struggled to entice churchgoers to return after the "virtual church" days of the COVID-19 pandemic, as many discovered they could have a similar experience through a TV or computer screen.[21]

But if our aim is to appeal to the *heart*, then the setting of our worship itself becomes an integral part of the overall experience. A church steeple can be a signpost that points people to pockets of beauty amidst an industrialized world stripped of it. How different might the world think of God if it saw those who worshipped Him as lovers and cultivators of beauty rather than of just doctrinal ideas and theological concepts?

3. Beauty in Life

In Fyodor Dostoevsky's novel *The Idiot,* Prince Lev Nikolayevich Myshkin famously declares, "Beauty will save the world."[22] The other characters dismiss the statement as naive, as might present-day readers (hence, the novel's title!). But that was the point. Beauty is deeper than a painting or flowerbed. What Dostoevsky had in mind was not material in form, but the immaterial beauty of Christian virtue.

Notably, as the popularity of the Christian church wanes in the wider culture, attraction toward Jesus remains strong.† In many ways,

---

† In a 2023 survey by Barna, 71 percent of Americans said they have positive opinions of Jesus, as opposed to only 47 percent saying the same of churches in their community. ("Openness to Jesus Isn't the Problem—the Church Is," Barna, May 17, 2023, www.barna.com/research /openness-to-jesus/.)

Jesus is more palpable to a Heart Culture than to a Head Culture. While many of His explosive truth claims face resistance by rational-minded skeptics, His character of love and grace and His elevation of the outcast or oppressed satisfy many of the highest ideals of the Heart Culture. Hildebrand notes, "The irresistible divine beauty of Jesus not only moves our will, but it attracts our heart."[23]

Jesus did not compromise truth in order to highlight beauty, and neither should we. Nevertheless, in adhering to the truth of Jesus, we should not overlook the *ways* of Jesus. As the Head Culture has shifted to a seemingly irrational Heart Culture, there has been a tendency for Christians to double down on the truth component, often at the expense of the beautiful. We have taken up Peter's challenge to give an answer to all who ask but may overlook the words that follow: "But do this with gentleness and respect, keeping a clear conscience, so that those who speak maliciously against your good behavior in Christ may be ashamed of their slander" (1 Pet. 3:15b–16). Truth is strengthened, not weakened, by grace and beauty.

In recent years, there has been pushback on the idea that Christians must be *winsome*. The notion invokes the image of a sleazy salesman with an artificial smile using charm to manipulate customers. That is not the example of Jesus. He was attractive not because of a put-on act but because His *life* radiated true beauty. He could stand against the winds of opposition as a pillar of grace, patience, and love.

Mother Teresa once said, "Do you want to do something beautiful for God? There is a person who needs you. This is your chance."[24] She spoke often of beauty, even if by most of today's cultural standards of smooth-skinned, unblemished youthfulness, her wrinkled and weathered face fell short. What she did was *live* beautifully. If God is the source of beauty, and the Spirit of God resides within every believer, then our lives should also bring pockets of beauty wherever we go.

Yearning for Beauty

One of the most profound moments in J. R. R. Tolkien's *The Lord of the Rings* comes when Frodo and Sam are in the dark, shadowy land of Mordor, near the end of their mission but too weary and discouraged to press on. In the moment of their greatest despair, Sam catches a glimpse of hope:

> There, peeping among the cloud-wrack above a dark
> tor high up in the mountains, Sam saw a white star
> twinkle for a while. The beauty of it smote his heart,
> as he looked up out of the forsaken land, and hope
> returned to him. For like a shaft, clear and cold, the
> thought pierced him that in the end the Shadow was
> only a small and passing thing: there was light and
> high beauty forever beyond its reach.[25]

Transcendent beauty exists, even if our clouded vision obscures it. In a shadowy world, where the ugly and artificial have become commonplace, a single glimpse of the beautiful can ignite something in our hearts. Jesus said we are the "light of the world" (Matt. 5:14–16), even as He is the "light of the world" (John 8:12).

A Heart Culture longs for beauty in an often unpleasant world. Like the orcs in Tolkien's tale, humans always face the temptation to tear down and destroy, only to discover that the resulting rubble offers nothing to satisfy our cravings. Such beauty is available only from above, in the objective reality of God's goodness and truth. As Christians, we point people to God—the ultimate source of all beauty—when we provide glimpses of that beauty through what we create and through the witness of our own lives.

Chapter 6

Art

We make ... because we are made: and not only made,
but made in the image and likeness of a Maker.

—J. R. R. Tolkien

The power of art is that it can connect us to one another, and to larger
truths about what it means to be alive and what it means to be human.

—Daniel Levitin

"That's Not Art!"

In 1926, the esteemed Romanian sculptor Constantin Brâncuși shipped several of his works to the United States for an exhibition. Among the collection was *Bird in Space*, a minimalist sculpture made of bronze. It was not until the completion of the voyage that things hit bumpy water. Upon arriving at the New York harbor, the cargo was unloaded and brought to customs. By law, all original works of art with "no practical purpose" are duty free. While all agreed that Brâncuși's creation had no practical purpose, the customs officials took one look at the piece and declared, "That's not art!"

The border agents deemed the work as a mere "manufactured metal object" and thus subject to the tariff of 40 percent of the sale price.

Brâncuşi obviously disagreed. After some heated words, the sculpture was eventually released on bond—under the bogus classification of "kitchen utensils and hospital supplies"—until final judgment could be made. Two years later, after a trial in which several art experts were brought in to testify, it was decreed that *Bird in Space* was indeed art and entitled to free entry.

In the end, Brâncuşi got the last laugh. The work is now widely acclaimed as a master-

Brâncuşi's studio at the Metropolitan Museum of Art in New York City

piece, and in 2005, a marble copy sold for $27,456,000, which was the highest price a sculpture had ever brought at auction at that time.[1]

Cheesecake Is Good, Actually

We are surrounded by art. From the films that fill our screens, to the latest must-read novel, to the songs that serenade us, to the images that adorn billboards and city walls, to the dancers gracing the ballet stage, to the storytellers on social media, to the rhythmic words of the poet on open-mic night, art is the unavoidable and often subliminal backdrop of our lives. Art is everywhere.

The omnipresence of art does not mean it is always appreciated or valued. The turbulent flight of *Bird in Space* is emblematic of how some perceive the creative arts as a subjective and largely trivial pleasure in which one person's worthless hunk of metal is another's masterpiece worth a staggering fortune. The Irish poet Oscar Wilde wrote, "All art is quite useless,"[2] and many pragmatic people might concur.* Psychologist Steven Pinker famously dismissed music as a sort of "auditory cheesecake," enjoyable but unnecessary, which could disappear from the world without making any significant difference (Pinker must be more of "a pie guy," since we believe the absence of cheesecake would make the world a significantly *worse* place).[3]

Christians might disagree with that assessment *in theory*, but our actions tell a different story. Sociologist Robert D. Putnam found that regular church attenders are more than twice as likely to volunteer in their communities as compared to non-church attenders. That disparity applied in every category of volunteering *except* for "arts and cultural organizations."[4]

We feature art—or, at least, *music*—in our services, but we can be largely indifferent to it outside our church walls. It remains a slice of cheesecake with some spiritual toppings. In order to effectively engage with a Heart Culture, we must reclaim the arts as an important part of our spiritual heritage. To speak the heart language is to speak through the creative arts.

It's a (He)Art Culture Out There

A Heart Culture is driven largely by the visual and aesthetic. In his prophetic book *Amusing Ourselves to Death*, Neil Postman perceived that the advent of television would shift the culture from word-centered

---

* The provocative words were not a disavowal of the arts (Wilde was an artist, after all), but a reflection on how art's value transcends practical use.

to image-centered.[5] Today, when complex ideas are simplified into internet memes and GIFs, his forecasts have proven true. The Heart Culture is an aesthetic culture, where the various creative arts pulsate with the beating hearts of the people.

The importance of the aesthetic dimension of culture is evident by where we direct our energy. In a Head Culture, Christians aimed their defense of the faith at atheist philosophers. In the Heart Culture, such efforts are instead often directed at entities like Disney and Netflix. The perceived agents of ideological change are no longer university professors but those who wield the power of the arts. Government buildings may be where social issues are legislated, but the great battles themselves are often waged through the art and entertainment of our culture. It's been aptly said that "Culture is the arts elevated to a set of beliefs."[†]

The arts receive plenty of blame for ushering in and propagating the current Heart Culture. But the power that has lured many spiritual wanderers off the path can also be used as a sweet sound to call them back. Amid an aesthetics-driven culture, Christians have a tremendous opportunity to speak the language of the heart through the arts.

The Arts Uncaged

Art and the church have a long and tempestuous history together. Novelist Dorothy Sayers wrote, "The Church as a body has never made up her mind about the Arts, and it is hardly too much to say that she has never tried."[6] The arts are a present element in most churches yet

---

† The quote is frequently attributed to author Thomas Wolfe, although like many popular quotes, the actual source proves elusive.

are often kept on a tight leash like a wild, exotic animal that captivates our imagination but is too dangerous to be let out of its cage. Taking a cue from Mary Poppins, we use the arts as a spoonful of sugar to help the medicine of preaching go down easier—but we are also quick to warn that sugar leads to cavities.

During our early college years, we both played guitar in a rock band. We never had much ambition beyond it being a fun hobby (well, and visions of a sold-out world tour), but we eventually had the opportunity to play some gigs, often in sketchy bars and other institutions we were not accustomed to visiting. We perceived these as opportunities to be a light in some dark places, but we weren't sure how. So we decided on giving a "Jesus talk," which was in vogue with Christian bands at the time. Near the end of the gig, we'd pause and share a brief statement about how we're Christians and how Jesus loves them, and then we'd get back to melting faces.

We're not sure if those Jesus talks did any harm (or good), but looking back, it does reveal our cautious approach to art. We wanted to communicate our faith in Christ but failed to see how we might do so outside a sermonette. We didn't trust the music to speak to the hearts of the audience, so we attempted to "baptize" our performances with a spiel aimed at their heads. Music was reduced to just the key to get us in the door and on a stage where we could preach (often to an unsuspecting audience who felt tricked rather than intrigued). In a sense, we were attempting to recreate church in the bar. All our band members had grown up in church, but we had never been discipled to see how our music could itself be a light.

In order to effectively engage with our Heart Culture, we must begin by reexamining the role of the arts—and stewardship of artists—within our churches. A church that speaks the language of the heart through the arts can accomplish this by embracing two important identities.

Identity One: Artistic Incubator

When confronted by a rational Head Culture, the church rose to the occasion to train its people to meet the need, leading to a widespread emphasis on apologetics. Now, faced with an aesthetically driven Heart Culture, how will we rise to the occasion? One possibility is to train those gifted in the arts to meet the current challenge.

On Christmas and Easter Sunday, many churches pull out all the stops. During these special occasions, stages are often graced with dancing and drama, and congregations may encounter poetry, flashy visuals, and various creative video components. On the "big event" Sundays, when churches are fuller than usual, we acknowledge that the arts have a valuable role to play, and we marshal our artists into action. But on that regular Sunday service in mid-October, the artists who do not sing or play an instrument are promptly put back in the storage closet for later.

We had one talented dancer tell us that she was blessed by the opportunity to share her talents with her church family, but she almost sheepishly admitted that she wished for more opportunities, and not just for those "special" services.

On another occasion, Daniel gathered twenty artists—painters, songwriters, screenwriters, dancers—in his home for fellowship and to share about their current artistic endeavors. By the end of the night, several had tears in their eyes, saying that it was the first time anyone had taken an interest in their creative passions. It wasn't only that the church didn't seem to give opportunities, but that most people in the church didn't even realize that people with such talents were sharing their pews. How many amazing, God-gifted artists are in our churches each week, and yet remain anonymous?

We remember watching a season of *American Idol* when the show was in its heyday and being surprised that eight of the top ten contestants professed some degree of Christian faith. Yet, the more we think about it, the less surprising it becomes. No other institution in America offers as open and regular an opportunity to sing as the church does. Music is an important part of our church identity, and thus, many learn the craft inside our walls.

What might our culture look like if our investment in filmmaking, writing, dance, and visual artistry matched our commitment to music?

We may be "people of the Book," but our Book is filled with the arts. When we open the Bible, we are met with song, poetry, and story. The arts are a part of our spiritual DNA. In a Heart Culture, the creative arts can be far more than a gimmick we deploy for a super-sized worship service. They should be a regular part of our communal worship, community outreach, and discipleship. Perhaps we would captivate the hearts of a creative and aesthetic generation more if they felt that church was fertile soil and congregations were water to help their gifts flourish.

The arts are sometimes decried as a double-edged sword. We recognize their value and gravitate to them and yet see examples of their negative influence all around us. The apostle Paul warned, "They exchanged the truth about God for a lie, and worshiped and served created things rather than the Creator" (Rom. 1:25a). Even God's own artistry can be used for sinful ends in the wrong hands. But surely that is no justification to avoid taking a nature walk and basking in the beauty of His created world. The potential abuse of the arts should not lead the church to leave the double-edged blade in its sheath but should motivate us to train up capable sword masters.

Identity Two: Artistic Launchpad

One year after a youth camp, our church brought many of the teenagers to the front of the congregation to share God's activity in their lives. Several felt the call to pastoral ministry, and a few even felt led to train and go as missionaries. The church celebrated, and rightfully so. After the service, one young man caught our attention. He was a recently graduated teenager who had attended camp but who had not shared publicly at the front that morning. We later found out that God had given him peace and direction to attend film school.

We've heard many church leaders decry the disproportionate amount of time people are immersed in the media and creative arts in contrast to their time spent in church.[‡] At the same time, churches tend to put much more emphasis on praising those whom God calls to church ministry than those whom God leads into other areas, including the creative arts. When we do emphasize the artistic calling, it is frequently for how the artists can contribute inside the church (e.g., worship pastor) rather than how the church can support the ministry

---

[‡] "Even using conservative estimates, the typical young person spends nearly twenty times more hours per year using screen-driven media than taking in spiritual content. And for the typical young churchgoer, the ratio is still more than ten times as much cultural content as spiritual intake." (David Kinnaman and Mark Matlock, *Faith for Exiles: 5 Ways for a New Generation to Follow Jesus in Digital Babylon* [Grand Rapids: Baker Books, 2019], 115.)

of the artist *outside* church programming. We spend our time warning young people about the dangerous influence of Hollywood rather than empowering them to bring their light into that world.

Christian artists have been aptly described as the preachers of general revelation.[7] When God revealed Himself, He did so through the special revelation of the Bible (2 Tim. 3:16) and the general revelation of His creation (Rom. 1:20). Preachers behind the pulpit fulfill the role of the first, but a need remains for the second—a role uniquely suited for artists.

The Bible is filled with memorable and heroic characters: mighty kings, bold prophets, fearless warriors, and devout disciples. Therefore, it might be surprising to learn that the first time Scripture mentions anyone being filled with the Spirit of God, it is not someone like that. That distinction is given to Bezalel and Oholiab, two artists and craftsmen (Ex. 31:2–6). God empowered them for the special assignment of building the tabernacle. Artists have a special role in communicating God's majesty to the world.

At the same time, being missional in our stewardship of artists is not just a task *for* the artists. We may speak of "Hollywood" as some sort of singular entity, but it is actually a network of many thousands of people, all fulfilling different roles. A director or actor may get credit for the latest blockbuster film, but more than a thousand people work on the production of those movies, with "artists" themselves making up a minority. Not all Christians are gifted artistically.[§] But the church

§ Although Mike and his artistic masterpiece *Stick Man Standing on Flat Ground* would beg to differ ...

can work in harmony to cultivate creativity inside their walls, then launch it out into the wider culture.

There was a young man in Mike's church who was given the opportunity to read one of his original poems as part of a testimony he shared at their Sunday service. The confidence he gained from that experience inspired him to enter a poetry night at a local cafe. When the church young adults heard about it, they relocated their weekly Bible study to that cafe to encourage him as he proclaimed his poetry—saturated with gospel hope—to a room full of captivated listeners.

Joining the Cultural Conversation

God is a divinely creative being. To describe God as "Creator" is not only to speak of what He *did* but of who He *is*. Due to many sensationalist cinematic portrayals, Armageddon is typically thought of as just the destruction of the old. "End of the world" movies spend most of their time focusing on destruction spectacle, but the actual "end of the world" story in the Bible is all about re-creation. God declared, "Behold, I make all things *new*" (Rev. 21:5 KJV). As Christians, we should embrace this biblical mindset.

In our cancel-culture society, we can be tempted to try to change and shape culture by subtraction rather than addition. We boycott more art than we create and criticize what exists rather than generate something new. A Heart Culture will not have their hearts shaped through censorship or boycotts. Hearts are captivated by discovering something new, something better. As Andy Crouch says, "The only way to change culture is to create more of it."[8]

The arts are cultural conversations in which society wrestles with new ideologies, explores hurts, seeks hope, and probes important questions. If those conversations have led to places we lament, perhaps part of the problem is that the church has too often stood on the outside, eavesdropping with arms crossed and head shaking, rather than being an active participant.

The beauty of the arts is that we can encounter them in many ways. They can comfort and unsettle, bring tears of joy or sadness, stretch our minds with complexity or capture them with simplicity. The arts are an extension of our humanity and encapsulate the full breadth of our experiences on this earth and our innate longing to reach beyond it. Let's look at four possibilities for the arts in a Heart Culture.

1. Art That Activates the Heart

Art can be used to stir the affections of the heart, not just as a vehicle to carry the intellectual messages of the head.

In his book *Republic*, Plato excludes artists from his ideal city-state because they wield such great power to inflame the heart and thus disrupt the stability he was aiming for.[9] One of the ways we attempt to "use" art, while keeping it safely tethered, is by insisting that the aesthetic qualities remain secondary and wholly subservient to the head.

This approach to art is like a public speaker who wants to add a visual component to his talk, so he includes a PowerPoint presentation with slides filled with bullet-point text. He is technically using a visual medium but not to its full potential. It remains a head appeal in an ill-fitting heart guise. This is the unfavorable reputation of many faith-based films, which can feel more like a Sunday school lesson hosted in a movie theater than something that sweeps you up in an immersive story.

At a breakout session of a Christian arts conference, Daniel eavesdropped on a conversation while attendees gave peer critiques of their book samples. An aspiring novelist declared to her partner, "But what's the *message*? That's the most important part. Your story needs to have a *message*." Interestingly, one of the most common critiques from Christians toward Hollywood is that their films are increasingly message-driven. We are repelled when the message usurps the artistry but are often guilty of supporting—or even demanding—the same approach when we agree with the message.

Like a parent sneaking spinach into a sugary muffin to get her picky child to eat it, such an approach may get bits of veggies into the child's stomach, but it doesn't instill a love for healthy food. And the instant the ruse is exposed, there is friction in the relationship. The arts are not just a heart way to smuggle in a head message. What art enables us to do is help people *feel* something. A sermon can activate the mind, but art can activate the heart.

A sermon can activate the mind,
but art can activate the heart.

Christians do not experience different emotions than unbelievers do. Nor is either group immune to the pains, hopes, and struggles of everyday life. Believers do, however, view these experiences in a different way. Much of the greatest art ever produced is religious art, but the subject matter of our art need not always be "religion." It should be *life*, but life as seen through the lens of the gospel.

The art we contribute to our culture can explore all the complex emotions and experiences of life. We can fill people with sorrow at a broken world and joy at simple blessings. We can wrestle with doubt and find comfort in unexpected hope. We can share our heartfelt stories as fellow pilgrims in a painful world, showing our scars as well as our treasures. We can create art out of the vulnerable, unfiltered, and raw truth of our hearts. Francis Schaeffer wrote, "A Christian should use these arts to the glory of God, not just as tracts, mind you, but as things of beauty to the praise of God. An art work can be a doxology in itself."[10]

2. Art That Aims the Heart

Art can be used to elevate the good, true, and beautiful and to direct our gaze toward them.

In Andrew Peterson's fantasy series, The Wingfeather Saga, Armulyn the Bard has traveled far and wide singing songs about the Shining Isle, the mythical lost Kingdom of Anniera across the sea. Although he has never seen the Isle with his eyes, his music keeps the memory of it alive: "There's a powerful magic in songs, you know. They can aim the heart, point it at what matters. My own heart has been aimed ever at the far horizon, and my feet have followed."[11] Peterson, who is also an accomplished musician, was no doubt inspired by his own experiences of how music contains an echo of heaven that draws us toward the sound.¶

¶ This book series has also been turned into a charming animated show by Angel Studios.

Music has spiritual power. In fact, Scottish composer Sir James MacMillan claimed that music is the most spiritual of the arts.[12] After all, there is an ephemeral quality to music; it exists only as it is being played. Friedrich Nietzsche, the same radical atheist who brashly declared "God is dead!" is alleged to have remarked that, "One who has completely forgotten Christianity truly hears it here as gospel," after hearing Bach's *St. Matthew Passion*.[13] Even famous atheist Richard Dawkins admitted that he still finds classic Christmas carols moving and detests their secular replacements (can you blame him?).[14]

We remember a conversation with an unbeliever who possessed a somewhat chilly demeanor. Unexpectedly, he revealed that every time he visited a church and heard gospel music play, he immediately became emotional to the point of fighting back tears. The man had been completely unmoved by rational explanations and sermons about faith. Yet in hearing gospel music wash over him, something stirred deep within his soul. The joyful music seeped through the cracks in his skepticism like a pleasant aroma hinting at the glory of the heavenly banquet table.

Music is not the only artistic medium that accomplishes this. A quote usually attributed to Pablo Picasso declares, "Art washes from the soul the dust of everyday life." Our art can till the hard ground of our hearts that are often saturated in things that are mundane, cynical, and uninspiring. Our art can ignite a sense of awe, wonder, and spiritual curiosity within skeptics. It can preserve God's truth, goodness, and beauty in a cultural landscape where such values are scarce. Not every work of art must have the immediate goal of "conversion." Sometimes, it is enough if it merely tilts our eyes heavenward.

3. Art That Unsettles the Heart

Art can be more than therapeutic comfort; it can also shake us out of our complacency and self-sufficiency.

One of Daniel's favorite artistic creations happens to be among the most controversial and reviled. *Immersion* (*Piss Christ*) is a 1987 photograph by American artist Andres Serrano. It depicts a crucifix submerged—as you might guess from the title—in urine.

Despite the outrage it sparked, Serrano, who is a professing Catholic, was attempting to make a profound point: that the crucifixion of Jesus has been reduced to a cheap trinket we wear around our necks. If we feel outraged at the defilement of a trinket, how much more should we detest our own sin heaped onto Jesus? Despite the ickiness of the picture, there is also beauty. The suffering Savior has not been diminished as a result of the defilement but remains in beautiful defiance of it.

The widespread aversion to *Immersion* reflects something about our expectation of art. When listening to the jingles of many Christian radio stations, words like "safe" and "encouraging" are cheerfully proclaimed as mantras. For Christians, art has sometimes been reduced to a form of therapeutic escapism defined by kitsch and sentimentality.

Dietrich von Hildebrand writes, "The characteristic of sentimentality is that the real theme is a certain softening, a delight in swimming in an ungenuine emotionality. The sentimental person never dedicates himself truly to the object. The object ... is not the theme but only a means to elicit a pseudo-emotion which the sentimental person enjoys."[15] We are drawn to art that pats us on the back and tells us it is going to be okay, leaving us comforted but largely unchanged and without much inspiration *to* change.

A biblical story that reveals God's sense of humor is when the Israelites are wandering in the desert and besieged by venomous snakes. For their salvation, God commanded Moses to make a staff that snake-bitten victims must look at—and ordered that the staff be in the shape of a snake (Num. 21:8)! A snake was the *last* thing the Israelites wanted to see at that moment. Why not a deer or butterfly? Perhaps because we all want something to comfort us, but sometimes what we need most is to be unsettled.

Rembrandt, the great Dutch painter, was a master at his art. In his era, his religious art was unusually visceral, both powerful and unsettling. His paint strokes infused the familiar biblical narratives with a shocking realism.

Interestingly, while many Christians are squeamish toward the horror genre, many of the great horror movie directors come from religious backgrounds. Religious creators know best the reality of spiritual darkness. We talked to one horror director who gushed about the amazing redemptive potential of the genre precisely *because* it disturbs us. "People are too comfortable today to ask important spiritual questions," he mused.

Christians should not stray too far from the reality of hope, but hope can only manifest where there is a felt need for it. In a world— and a church—that offers countless ways to insulate and comfort us, one of the most powerful uses of the arts is to disrupt our sense of security. We can use the creative arts to invoke a healthy unsettling and discontent, tapping into the powerful emotions that most of us repress or avoid. Through art, the church has an opportunity to probe uncomfortable emotions in order to remind us of our desperate need for God's salvation.

4. Art That Illuminates the Heart

Art can be used to communicate gospel truth in a broader way.

Long ago, when a student failed to respond well to classical auditory teaching methods, he or she would be labeled a "dunce."** Fortunately, due to advances in pedagogical research, teachers now understand that not all students learn the same way. There are auditory learners, visual

learners, and kinesthetic learners. Teachers know they cannot communicate through just one style and expect a diverse collection of individuals to all benefit. While we have made progress in our educational system, have we learned the same lesson in our churches?

The verbal proclamation of the Word has a celebrated position in our churches, as it should. But are we intentionally communicating in ways that

The east window of St Michael and All Angels
Church, Southwick, West Sussex.

appeal to all? Or do we stick with the way that might be most natural and familiar to us?

One of the original functions of religious art was to proclaim the Bible to an illiterate culture. Stained-glass windows and sculptures

---

** Daniel once had "boo hiss" written in bold red ink on his college midterm, although unfortunately not for any outdated pedagogical mindset, but merely the result of his own blundering incompetence!

displayed outside cathedrals depicted biblical scenes for a society unable to read the Bible for themselves. Today, in a biblically illiterate and "image-centric" Heart Culture, art can serve a similar function, giving form to abstract theology and allowing biblical truth to be communicated in a tangible way.

At Mike's church, an artist paints offstage during the service, giving visual expression to the themes of the worship gathering. Afterward, he presents the artwork to the congregation. Art from previous weeks is also displayed throughout the room, providing a visual testimony of the biblical truths the church has been exploring. Another man in his church hosts a weekly gathering in his apartment with neighbors, representing a wide spectrum of religious belief. They share dinner together and watch a TV show depicting the life of Jesus. They follow each episode with a discussion of what they saw, referring to their Bibles to further explore the questions that arose in their hearts through the visual experience.

When approaching a biblical narrative, why not dip into the vast ocean of the Christian artistic tradition? Some of the most creatively gifted men and women in history have wrestled with those scriptural narratives in striking ways. The poet Emily Dickinson wrote, "Tell the truth, but tell it slant."[16] The arts don't detract from our presentation of truth—they allow us to see it from a new angle.

Art in the World

Before becoming an artist, Vincent envisioned a different career path. As a young man, he trained for the pastorate before being rejected. Next, he lived as a missionary but was once again dismissed (not for any misconduct, but for wishing to live humbly among the people in a way deemed "undignified" by the religious leaders). Thus, he went through door number three—and became a painter.

In his most famous painting, *The Starry Night*, the starlit sky swirls with almost spectral beauty. Below, other lights shine from the

windows of the houses. But in the middle of the painting is one building with no light: the church. Despite occupying a central position in the canvas, it is dark and almost lost among the beauty surrounding it. The painting seems to represent the disconnect between the artist

Starry Night

and the established church, while on a wider level, it reveals the potential for the artist to bring that beauty into the world.[††]

In a Heart Culture driven by the aesthetic and increasingly saturated in art and media, perhaps the loudest megaphone from which we can speak is through the arts. By fostering a culture of creativity within our walls, we can speak to those enticed by the aesthetic and equip the God-gifted creatives to uniquely take gospel hope into the world.

[††] For a stimulating interpretation of van Gogh's *The Starry Night,* see Makoto Fujimura, *Culture Care: Reconnecting with Beauty for our Common Life* (Downers Grove, IL: IVP Books, 2017), 74–77.

Chapter 7

Desire

*This infinite abyss can be filled only with an
infinite and immutable object;
in other words by God himself.*

—Blaise Pascal

*It seems to me that if secularism is going to be a positive creed, it
can't just speak to the rational aspects of our nature. Secularism has
to do for nonbelievers what religion does for believers—arouse the
higher emotions, exalt the passions in pursuit of moral action.*

—David Brooks

Secular Religiosity

Geek conventions are a fascinating phenomenon. In the eighties,
Belinda Carlisle sang that "Heaven Is a Place on Earth," but for many
people today—particularly introverts and non-geeks—events like
the San Diego Comic-Con may look more like an acute manifesta-
tion of hell.

Each year, thousands of people descend upon these convention
halls, traveling across the country and bunking a dozen to a hotel
room to make a sacred pilgrimage to the holy center of Geekdom.

These pilgrims will stand in line for hours, then crowd like sardines into a room to be among the first to view a new movie trailer that will be released on YouTube later that day—and max out credit cards to purchase merchandise that is likely cheaper and more conveniently bought online.

To someone looking upon the madness from the outside, it seems like foolishness. And yet, the more you come to understand human nature, the more Comic-Con not only makes sense, but—like Thanos—is almost inevitable.

We jokingly used religious language above, but that's probably not much of an exaggeration. Esteemed movie critic Leonard Maltin once mused: "I've always regarded movie going as a kind of religious experience."[1] In many ways, fandoms are quasi-religious communities. They offer a sense of identity, ignite our loves, and stir up feelings of emotional ecstasy. A person can enjoy something alone, but doing so while aligning yourself with a group evokes a sense of belonging to something larger than yourself.

Events like geek conventions exist because humans are passionate beings full of powerful desires, and we're all looking to satisfy them and allow them to flourish.

In Neil Gaiman's novel *American Gods*, he weaves an imaginative picture of this reality. In his story, the "Old Gods" of mythology have faded away, only to be replaced by new deities. Unlike the former gods—who came to earth from the beyond—the "New Gods" derive their existence and power from being personifications of the current passions, loves, and desires of America (media, technology, Wall Street, etc.).

Despite a world that outwardly appears to be abandoning traditional religious deities, humans have an innate urge to worship, so we inevitably create new spiritual guides in their place. Gaiman notes, "The modern gods right now are the things we give our attention to, the things that we give our time to, because time is precious, time is what we use to worship."[2]

We all have desires that motivate us, and we all cultivate those passions. The only question is *how*. For Christians to speak the language of a Heart Culture, our message must intersect with the desires that drive people from the inside. To speak the heart language is to speak the language of desire.

What We Desire (and How We Satisfy It)

In a Heart Culture, passion is often a higher virtue than restraint, and *what* you believe is less important than how zealously you pursue it. However, perhaps these assumptions focus on the symptoms rather than the cause. After all, exterior passion and emotion are the outworking of our inner desires.

The Pixar film *Inside Out* tells a story about a young girl named Riley as she adjusts to her family's move to a new city. The real plot, however, is all the action going on "behind the scenes" and the internal adventures of her personified emotions—Joy, Anger, Disgust, Sadness, and Fear. This charming movie captures a profound truth: what we see on the outside is a small reflection of a whole complicated world beneath the surface.

God designed us with desires. We may disagree with the manner in which people seek to gratify these desires, but we must admit that it is natural to pursue them. A child may express a need for food through an explosion of tears and wails, but there is nothing abnormal about the desire to be fed. That is how we were created. As we grow and mature, we (hopefully) learn to satisfy these cravings without emotional outbursts. But if you've ever had a coworker or classmate who missed a meal, you know that those childlike, emotional responses to unsatisfied hunger can reappear!*

Issues of identity dominate the discourse today. We may not like the direction those conversations sometimes go, but it is natural for us to want to understand who we are. Activism permeates all corners of society, and though we may not endorse some of it, it is natural for humans to seek purpose. Christians may bemoan the secular idols, but it is natural for us to long for transcendence as beings created to worship. The issue in a Heart Culture is not that people have desires but that those desires are unsatisfied, and unfulfilled desires spawn emotional responses.

In *Mere Christianity*, C. S. Lewis put it this way:

> Creatures are not born with desires unless satisfaction for those desires exists. A baby feels hunger: well, there is such a thing as food. A duckling wants to swim: well, there is such a thing as water. Men feel sexual desire: well, there is such a thing as sex. If I find in myself a desire which no experience in this world can satisfy, the most probable explanation is that I was made for another world.[3]

Similarly, Saint Augustine said, "You have made us for yourself, and our heart is restless until it rests in you."[4]

---

* Some of the best marriage advice we ever heard was simply "Always carry a granola bar!"

Instead of "emotional," a better word to describe the Heart Culture may be "restless." People are filled with desires that can be satisfied only in Christ. And yet they continue to hunt for satisfaction in the world, finding temporary emotional highs but nothing of transcendent value.

Make Them Wish It Were True

Christians have an incredible redemptive opportunity to guide the restless souls of our Heart Culture to where they can find relief (Matt. 11:28–29). Jesus declared that He is the lasting answer to our needs: "I am the bread of life. Whoever comes to me will never go hungry, and whoever believes in me will never be thirsty" (John 6:35). Instead of condemning the passions of the Heart Culture, we can demonstrate how those desires are properly satisfied only in Jesus.

Blaise Pascal put it like this:

> Men despise religion. They hate it and are afraid it may be true. The cure for this is first to show that religion is not contrary to reason, but worthy of reverence and respect. Next make it attractive, make good men wish it were true, and then show that it is. Worthy of reverence because it really understands human nature. Attractive because it promises true good.[5]

To "make it attractive" does not mean to manufacture a false or misleading appeal for the gospel. Rather, it means to help people understand that Christ is the answer they have unknowingly desired all along. Not "contrary to reason" (the popular criticism of skeptics), but truly meeting the desires of our human nature.

Does our culture see the Christian faith as irrelevant—or even antithetical—to their innate desires? Is church perceived as a place where the yearnings of the heart are abandoned or fulfilled? Note the words Pascal used for what keeps people at bay: *despise, hate, afraid.* These are heart responses to something they don't truly understand. Christians can "make it attractive" by making sense of the desires that drive these emotional reactions.

The Ultimate Desire

In the Disney classic *Cinderella*, as the heroine dances with Prince Charming for the first time, she sings, "So this is love. So this is what makes life divine.... The key to all heaven is mine. My heart has wings, and I can fly."[6] Disney stories are rarely the best guides for realistic romance, although we like to think that our own wives sang similar lyrics after meeting us. In *Cinderella*, the rags-to-riches princess is actually touching on a deep, theological point. The desire for—and satisfaction of—love is where our hearts intersect with the divine.

The Bible says, "Whoever does not love does not know God, because God is love" (1 John 4:8). To know God is to love Him and be loved by Him. While Cinderella's romantic euphoria may be a distant echo of that divine love, it is driven by the same deeply rooted desire. In fact, when the Bible speaks about the relationship between God and His people, marriage is the most common metaphor used.[7] Jesus said that the greatest commandments are to "love the Lord your God" and "love your neighbor as yourself," for "all the Law and the Prophets hang on these two" (Matt. 22:36–40).

Imagine our human desires as a tree. We have many branches but only one trunk, which is fed by roots beneath the earth. The trunk of the tree is *love*. It is the core of who we are: beings who love and who desire to be loved. All our other desires—identity, purpose, transcendence—are expressions of this main desire branching out from the trunk. Therefore, the important question is: "What feeds the trunk?"

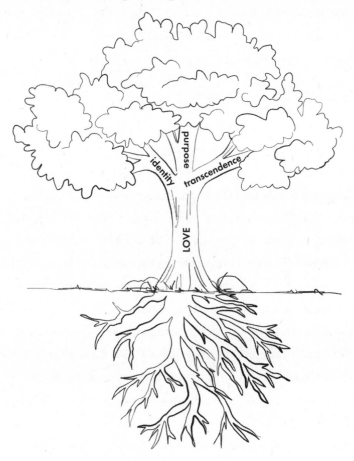

James K. A. Smith writes, "To be human is to have a heart. You can't not love. So the question isn't *whether* you will love something

as ultimate; the question is *what* you will love as ultimate."[8] What we love as ultimate is where we hope to find life—the roots that feed the rest of the tree. A pile of disconnected branches is suited for starting a fire, but the branches are dead and unable to grow apart from connection to a root source. Our ultimate desire—love—gives life to the other desires of our hearts. Thus, the roots that give life to the trunk will impact the full tree.

> The issue in a Heart Culture is not
> that people have desires but that
> those desires are unsatisfied.

For many people in the West, the most famous verse in the Bible is John 3:16. That verse is an incredible reminder that God's love for us is what gives us life. Through Christ, the trunk is fed and will give life and direction to all the other desires that branch out from it. When Christians are called to love others, it is not just to make people feel good or welcome in our worship services. Love is not a preamble; it is the main event. It is God's invitation to nourish the core of who we are by loving others as Jesus loved us (John 13:34). Cultivating this love will work itself into satisfying all the other desires of our hearts.

Three Desires

The human heart is filled with many desires, both conscious and subconscious. Some are held in harmony, while others seem to contradict each other. In a Heart Culture, there are at least three key desires: identity (who we are), purpose (why we are), and transcendence (what we are). Let's explore how we can speak the heart language into each of these.

Desire 1: Identity

What It Is

There's a quote usually attributed to philosopher William James that says: "Whenever two people meet, there are really six people present. There is each man as he sees himself, each man as the other person sees him, and each man as he really is."

No desire is more central or easy to perceive in the current Heart Culture than the desire for identity. "Who am I?" is one of the primary questions of the current age. From the fervent LGBTQ+ discussion, to the theme of "racial diversity" in Hollywood, to the political tribalism lighting up social media, many of the important cultural conversations center on the desire to establish an identity and have others affirm it.

We've heard the phrase "Wherever you go, there you are." Identity is an attempt to understand that ever-present self we live with every second of every day. Your identity may be a constant comfort or a nagging doubt, but more likely it is a continual and evolving conversation that you're seeking clarity in. Paradoxically, a society that seems to rebel against "labels" has generated new labels at an exponential rate. Our Heart Culture is continuing to expand the guidelines for establishing an identity, and in the process making that task more and more elusive, confusing, and disheartening.

How to Appeal to It

The church has not been silent on speaking to this desire, but the way we have done so has sometimes been unintentionally dismissive and counterproductive.

Once, while traveling and visiting a new church, Mike heard a Sunday school teacher declare, "I am not an American. I am not white. I am not a husband. I am not a father. I am a *Christian*. That is the only label that matters." This proclamation certainly would have been unexpected news to his three daughters sitting beside him (although perhaps that takes them off the hook to buy a Father's Day gift!). Mike knew he was well-meaning, and he understood the point he was making, but the reality is the man was *all* of those things. He also watched the eyes of a predominantly young adult audience begin to glaze over, as rather than speak to the issues that mattered to them, the teacher dismissed those questions as irrelevant.

Faith is foundational, but it is not the only distinguishing aspect of our identity. Christ isn't the replacement for all other characteristics—He is the lens through which we see them most clearly. In John's vision of heaven, he saw "a great multitude that no one could number, from every nation, from all tribes and peoples and languages, standing before the throne" (Rev. 7:9 ESV). The identity of Christ will bring everyone to the throne room of heaven, and yet the crowd will not become an indistinguishable blur; it will remain a beautiful mosaic.

In Galatians 3:27-28, the apostle Paul pinpointed three sources of identity that remain relevant today: race, gender, and social status. While asserting that Christ is a new label that we "put on," Paul does not dismiss the reality of these other identities. He wrote, "There is neither Jew nor Gentile," but he also identified himself as a Jewish missionary to Gentiles. He said, "Nor is there male and female," but also provided instruction specifically to males and females. He wrote that there is "neither slave nor free," but he also penned a letter to the slave-owner Philemon on the topic of his runaway slave.

It may not resonate with a Heart Culture if we point to the gospel as an answer that puts a hard end to all subsequent questions of identity. Questions of gender, race, and social status are common because they are held to be of high importance. Though these labels can be divisive, evidenced by the vitriol that often accompanies them, the beauty of the Christian message is that the Christ label is a unifier that connects and makes sense of all the other ways we understand ourselves.

The question of identity can be an individualistic pursuit, but the goal of "identity politics" is often to position oneself within a group. The label that the Christian faith offers is one that unifies those from across any number of separate tribal groups into something we have in common. As Paul said, "For *as many of you* as were baptized into Christ have *put on* Christ" (Gal. 3:27 ESV).

Desire 2: Purpose

What It Is

We remember when movie fans bought tickets to see *Avengers: Endgame* (2019) multiple times—some people boasting of hitting double digits—to catapult it up the charts for a chance of becoming the all-time highest box office grossing film, in pursuit of *Avatar* (2009).

Amusingly, both films were owned by Disney. Whichever movie won that contest, Disney was the true winner. The competition was ultimately trivial, and even those who contributed to the race likely did not rest their long-term hopes and dreams on the outcome. But it became a cultural moment because it offered an undemanding chance for people to devote themselves to a cause—and thus a purpose toward which to direct their actions.

People long for purpose. This desire is evident in many ways, from passionate climate activism, to political protests, to the organized "canceling" of those deemed to represent harmful ideologies. Advertisers have also keyed in on this truth, realizing that it is more effective to sell a purpose than a product. To buy a candy bar or tub of ice cream today is no longer to just get yummy goodness inside you. Now it's also an act of support for a humanitarian or activist cause, which becomes the central feature in the marketing campaign.

Heart Culture citizens are driven to rally around a purpose. In multiple surveys of Gen Z, the desire to make a positive difference in the world consistently rises near the top. We may differ on the definition of "positive," but there is no denying that our Heart Culture is trying to make a difference, and this serves as a guiding purpose for their actions.

How to Appeal to It

The desire for purpose can be misdiagnosed by the church. In trying to keep young people engaged in church, we can fall back (sometimes unintentionally) on entertainment. In an age of what Tony Reinke calls "Competing Spectacles," we are contending with countless other displays vying for people's attention.[9] When our goal is to draw people into church (or keep them from leaving), we are tempted to come up with big events or to increase the budget to elevate the visual stage production.

A church leader in a city with a high concentration of creatives and a hub for performances once told us, "People have high expectations. They're accustomed to excellence on stage. That's who we're competing with for their attention." And yet, there is only a competition if the two parties vying for people's attention are offering the same product. Secular culture can saturate the market with entertainment, but the church can offer something more. It can offer *purpose.*

We may seek to keep teenagers entertained, but when those young adults graduate high school, they are not satisfied with Youth Group 2.0. They are seeking their purpose. We can't afford to fill their schedules but not their hearts.

Instead of multiplying church programming and rallies, what if we invited young people into active service—not just as available volunteers for church events but also as active participants in their community?

The desire for purpose does not beat only in the hearts of young people stepping into their independence. Adults in the workforce, the elderly who have retired, and stay-at-home parents hoping to shape the future for their children all share the core desire for their lives to contribute to something bigger. We may decry a consumer mindset of churchgoers and yet enable it by offering programming to consume rather than a platform to actively participate in the Christian mission.

To speak to a Heart Culture, we must challenge people by offering a higher purpose for their lives. They want to make a tangible difference in the world, and if the church offers only a passive experience, then they will look to satisfy this desire somewhere else. Jesus consistently taught His followers to take their eyes off themselves to fulfill their calling to love their neighbors in practical ways (Matt. 25:31–46). God has purposes that have been prepared for us since long before we were born (Eph. 2:10). What if our churches helped the culture discover this reality?

Desire 3: Transcendence

What It Is

Cinema once promised a gateway for a transcendent experience, an escape from our material lives. Of the sixty top-earning movies of all time, only *seven* lack clear fantastical elements (magic, superpowers, imaginary creatures and worlds).

On a wider level, the experience of cinema itself might fill our desire for transcendence. This is why we guard ourselves against spoilers before a much-anticipated movie comes out. We want to preserve a sort of heightened experience. In fact, psychologists have found that the human body actually produces dopamine (a "feel-good" hormone) in anticipation of pleasure, not only when experiencing it. James Clear notes, "Your brain has far more neural circuitry allocated for *wanting* rewards than for *liking* them."[10] We are constantly seeking a heightened experience, even if the experience itself rarely lives up to the hype.

There's a scene in *Jurassic World* (2015) where a kid is mere feet away from a dinosaur that is feeding but turns away in boredom. When contrasted with the overwhelming awe and wonder the characters experience at the first sight of the dinosaurs in Spielberg's original *Jurassic Park* (1993), the moment becomes a meta commentary for audiences. We have become desensitized toward the spectacles that once excited us.[†] So we turn our attention toward bigger and newer thrills in our desire to experience something that elevates us beyond our mundane lives.

This is why the "Nones" demographic remains largely spiritual in orientation, even as it spurns traditional religions. They may wish to rid themselves of religious institutions, but they can't shake the deeply rooted desire for transcendence. Sam Harris, one of the leaders in the New Atheist movement, remains firmly atheistic but has rebranded himself a sort of guru for meditative practices.[‡] His head rejects the existence of God, but his heart still longs for a transcendent replacement.

An interesting trend among those who leave the Christian faith is how quickly their replacement comes to resemble what they left. For deconstructionists who reject their prior religious establishments and traditions, their movement has formed into a parallel religious community.[§] There are gurus and prophets to guide others through the deconstruction process. There are creeds and shared language and even physical gatherings of like-minded communities. In fact, some atheist groups have attempted to put on weekly services with all the hallmarks of traditional church, including music, moral teachings, contemplation, and fellowship.[¶]

[†] Let's just say, the entire Jurassic World "sequel trilogy" inspired a similar reaction from us.

[‡] He gives voice to this most clearly in his book *Waking Up: A Guide to Spirituality without Religion*.

[§] Some have branded themselves "Ex-vangelicals."

[¶] One such expression is the Sunday Assembly, a secular version of "church" founded in London in 2013, and now boasting several thousand members globally. ("What Are Atheist Churches?," *The Week*, last updated May 21, 2018, www.theweek.co.uk/93733/what-are-atheist-churches.)

In other words, those antagonistic or apathetic toward Christianity are unable to fully repress their need to worship and satisfy their God-instilled desires. They are those who look at our Christian faith and conclude that the world provides better hope than the church in satisfying those needs. David Brooks summarizes the situation this way:

> The only secularism that can really arouse moral motivation and impel action is an enchanted secularism, one that puts emotional relations first and autonomy second. I suspect that over the next years secularism will change its face and become hotter and more consuming, less content with mere benevolence, and more responsive to the spiritual urge in each of us, the drive for purity, self-transcendence and sanctification.[11]

How to Appeal to It

God has "set eternity in the human heart; yet no one can fathom what God has done from beginning to end" (Eccl. 3:11). Transcendence is a spiritual homing beacon that urges wayward travelers back home. C. S. Lewis popularized the German word *sehnsucht* to describe this sensation. The word means "yearning" or "wistful longing." Lewis himself described it as "that unnameable something, desire for which pierces us like a rapier."[12] It is a healthy discontent, a sense in our soul that aims us toward greater spiritual realities that we don't fully comprehend.

Other theologians have discerned a similar reality. Pascal described it as an "infinite abyss."[13] Alvin Plantinga (building on John Calvin) spoke of a *sensus divinitatis* (Latin for "sense of divinity") within each of us.[14] Rudolf Otto wrote of a "numinous" experience: "the presence of that which is a *Mystery* inexpressible and above all creatures."[15]

In the church, there can be a perception that cultural engagement begins on a completely blank slate—that we must first create a demand before we can provide the supply. We tend to think that we in the church, like the characters in Christopher Nolan's sci-fi movie *Inception*, must first labor to somehow implant a yearning for our spiritual message within the hearts of unbelievers before we can offer the gospel to meet this newfound need.

In a Heart Culture, perhaps it is better to begin with a conviction that the heart of every person is *already* being stirred and pulled toward the divine. We don't need to convince someone that she desires transcendence; we need to show her how God fills the need she already recognizes within herself.

One way to appeal to this desire is to not be bashful about the transcendent realities of faith. In a well-meaning attempt to be "seeker sensitive," we can narrowly focus our message on so-called practical topics or immediate needs, to the point that our Christian communities appear more as self-help groups with some Jesus sprinkled in than an entrance into the throne room of a divine Creator.

Churches *should* demonstrate how faith intersects with practical pursuits—that's the point we're exploring in this chapter. And yet, if one of our heartfelt needs is a desire for something *beyond* our everyday experience, then we should be careful not to make our message so "practical" that it loses its unique relevance in the midst of a bloated self-help industry.

The world apart from Christ cannot satiate our internal longing and desire for transcendence. In how we speak of God and how we come together into His holy presence to worship, we can open our hearts—and the hearts of those around us—to a transcendent experience, an echo from Eden that reminds us of a paradise lost and a veiled glimpse of the eternal splendor just beyond our mortal reach that we will one day call home.

Conclusion

A Heart Culture is a messy and confusing world where restless people seek to fulfill desires they cannot fully fathom and look for satisfaction in places that never satiate their needs. The culture is widely characterized by emotional outbursts and destructive desires. This should not surprise us. It should break our hearts more than inflame our anger. For we are all instilled with desires by God, and to leave them unmet is a dehumanizing experience. Like a nagging itch, the Heart Culture scratches with increased vigor, sharp nails opening hurtful wounds, but still unable to find relief.

Antoine de Saint-Exupéry once stated, "If you want to build a ship ... don't drum up people to collect wood and don't assign them tasks and work, but rather teach them to long for the endless immensity of the sea."[16]

For those being tossed upon the waves of a Heart Culture, maybe what they need most is not a well-rehearsed lecture or detailed step-by-step outline of what awaits them on the other side of the

tempestuous ocean of faith. Many traditional approaches to evangelism take this mindset, proclaiming the heavenly paradise that awaits
Christians in the *future*. Perhaps we can seek to provide a glimpse—
faint as it may be—of its splendor, igniting a fire that reorients the
bearing of their life in *this* world and draws them onward to pursue
that distant shore.

Chapter 8

Community

We expect more from technology and less from each other.
—Sherry Turkle

The culture is most dramatically engaged by the
church presenting it with another culture, another
form of community, rooted in her liturgical worship
practices and manifested in the loving community
that exists both in and beyond the worship service.
—Carl R. Trueman

Housecoats and Parking Lot Sword Fights

The clock approached midnight on May 19, 2005. The two of us, along with a group of friends and hundreds of other nerds, crowded the parking lot of our local movie theater vying to be among the first to experience *Star Wars III: Revenge of the Sith*. We grew up as "Star Wars kids." The original trilogy were the first live-action films we ever watched. Now we were teenagers, but our hearts had never left behind that galaxy far, far away.

Showings were staggered by mere minutes (12:01, 12:02, 12:03, etc.) so that the masses of wannabe Jedi could experience the cinematic story at the same time. The doors didn't open until closer to the showtime, so the parking lot was crammed with fans in eager anticipation. There were more housecoats here than all the city's church nativity plays combined, as fans showcased their homemade cosplay outfits. All of a sudden, the darkness lit up with a dazzling display of a hundred toy lightsabers, as an impromptu galactic battle began.

Once we finally made it inside and found our seats, two of our more extroverted friends put on a display of their "swordsmanship" at the front of the theater, to the cheers of the hyped-up audience. When the iconic opening crawl splashed across the screen, it was greeted with applause, then hushed silence, as we all united in our shared experience of a common love.

It was unforgettable. Even years later, when crossing paths with those "sword-fighting" friends again, we laugh while reminiscing about that night. What's ironic is that we all thought the actual movie was *terrible*! But that fact is relegated to a footnote in our memories because it was never truly about a geeky space opera. It was about the energy, excitement, and camaraderie. Our experience exemplified one of the most powerful yearnings of the human heart: a desire for community.

Craving Community

Human beings are wired to be relational. Extroverted or introverted, we all desire community; we merely seek it in differing ways.*

---

* Susan Cain debunks the myth that introverts are "antisocial" in her book *Quiet: The Power of Introverts in a World That Can't Stop Talking* (New York: Broadway Books, 2013).

Psychologist Jonathan Haidt notes, "We need others to complete us. We are an ultrasocial species, full of emotions finely tuned for loving, befriending, helping, sharing, and otherwise intertwining our lives with others."[1]

Community is the workshop where the various individual pieces of our private lives are fashioned into an identity. We define ourselves largely by which communities we belong to. That is why even our most private and personal identifiers—from sexuality to musical tastes— inevitably compel us to align with (or against) others, since we only truly understand who we are through relational connections.

The Heart Culture aches for community and belonging. It is one of their defining values, a root cause that gives life to many of the primary cultural concerns of our day—political divisiveness, sexual revolution, social justice, and distrust of traditional institutions. To speak the heart language today is to speak the language of community. It is to perceive the yearning that drives people and to recognize that this need can ultimately be fulfilled by Jesus and His church. It is a need that cannot be met by a sixty-second meet-and-greet after the church announcements. Rather, it requires us to be a life-giving community amid a lonely and divided world.

The Disappearance of Community

The younger generation is sometimes dismissed as antisocial because of the time they spend connected to technology (which, of course, is not just a young-person issue). But this is to misdiagnose the malady. The myth of the antisocial generation was challenged in the aftermath of the COVID-19 pandemic lockdowns. Data revealed that depression diagnoses skyrocketed and, perhaps surprisingly, those hit hardest were in the young-adult demographic.[2] Before the pandemic, it was assumed that digital communication tools had replaced traditional social connections for this group. However, during the pandemic, these young people still had access to all those same tools—and yet they felt the loss of physical community as deeply as anyone.

The Heart Culture has not lost its primal desire for community, but we are living in a world that can make satisfying that desire more difficult. This reality is not just affecting the younger generation. David Kinnaman and Mark Matlock observe, "Data shows that adults are twice as likely to say they are lonely compared to a decade ago; about one out of five Americans say they feel lonely."[3] In other words, we are more unsocialized than antisocial. We still desire community, but we're increasingly less able to find it.

In his insightful book *Bowling Alone,* sociologist Robert D. Putnam observed that while people in America continued to participate in leisure activities, they were doing so less *together.* Social bonds—the "glue" that holds society together—have weakened. As church attendance wanes, many traditional social meeting spots fade, and families are increasingly broken, a Heart Culture is left to navigate a world that has become unglued.

A technological ecosystem gives the illusion of community, but it is often a mirage. As a result, we live in a culture that is paradoxically more global and connected than any time in human history, and also more depressed and lonely.

The Oscars and the Church

Let's be honest: the Academy Awards ceremony is rarely riveting entertainment. Obscure movies are celebrated (then instantly forgotten), and celebrities parade across the stage to preach whatever trendy ideology or activist cause is in vogue that year. However, as we watched one of the recent ceremonies, we had an epiphany: the utopia yearned for by Hollywood's self-proclaimed prophets sounded an awful lot like the Christian church.

Hollywood celebrities were painting an idyllic vision of a diverse and united world where people are treated equally, rather than being segregated by social labels, where the most vulnerable have their needs met, and where communities link arms to stand for justice and against oppression. Hollywood has a reputation for recycling ideas, and in this, they are merely repackaging the community that Jesus called His followers to cultivate. The culture is expressing a need that Jesus established the church to meet.

The church is called to more than just having an answer; we are called to *be* the answer. The first church was a countercultural movement that transcended social, racial, and gender distinctions. Many of the first converts were social outcasts and misfits. Christians offered a unified and diverse community, a unique answer to the need for belonging. The Heart Culture of today is different from that of the first century, but the need for community remains, and the church is still God's answer.

Trust Lost and Earned

The church may be God's answer, but a Heart Culture is hesitant to seek us out with their questions. One of the primary challenges for the church to meet the culture's needs is the accumulated baggage. While a Heart Culture desires community, there is an acute distrust of institutions—and the church is high on that list.

Years ago, a spoken-word video on YouTube entitled "Why I Hate Religion, but Love Jesus" went viral, amassing more than 35 million views.[4] The poet—Jefferson Bethke—differentiated religion from the church, yet the current trend is to see the two as synonymous. A Barna survey found that roughly 10 percent of Americans fall into the category, "Love Jesus but not the Church."[5]

Daniel witnessed this sobering trend firsthand when he asked a classroom of nearly forty high school students if they believed the church was an important part of the Christian faith. Only three raised their hands. For those of us in the church, we may declare the slogan that "Christianity is not a religion—it's a relationship," but many in a Heart Culture see the church as a religion that cannot satisfy their need *for* relationships.

> The Heart Culture of today is different
> from that of the first century, but the
> need for community remains, and
> the church is still God's answer.

Trust is easily lost but difficult to gain back. Many people who have rejected the Christian faith have been motivated by an unwelcoming, hostile, or abusive experience in the church. We must earn back the trust of the culture by living in accordance with our calling as Christians, both inside the walls of our sacred spaces and as citizens of the wider communities where God has placed us. Let's explore five areas where the church intersects with the Heart Culture's yearning for community.

Christian Community in a Heart Culture
1. A Lonely World (Companionship)

Social Ties

We in the church resist the criticism that we are merely a social club. But that effort can lead to us downplaying the social dimension of church. Many social events are "baptized" with spiritual elements or a tacked-on devotional, seemingly to justify the gathering—as though Christians gathering together to laugh and fellowship is an insufficient reason. If we understand ourselves and our world largely in the context of community, then the fellowship aspect of our churches is vitally important.

In fact, theology might not play as big a role in drawing people into Christian community as we might assume. Theology is important, and the church is more than a social club. But while people in a Head Culture may have been primarily interested in the content of our doctrine, many in a Heart Culture are primarily seeking a place of belonging.

"Doctrine plays a very secondary role in conversion," notes sociologist Rodney Stark. "People convert when their social ties to members of a religious group outweigh their ties to nonmembers."[6] Stark is observing from a sociological perspective and does not take into account the active work of God to draw people to Jesus (John 6:44). Nevertheless, he highlights the important role relationships play when one is wavering between two different communities: the church and the world.

From Horizontal to Vertical

In 2023, the US surgeon general focused on what he declared to be "our epidemic of loneliness and isolation."[7] For many people, the most immediate concerns are not the big, existential questions of life, but

merely finding a way to alleviate their loneliness. Before they are ready
to accept doctrine about a divine Creator in heaven, they simply want
to feel seen in the physical world around them. They are looking for
"horizontal" relationships before "vertical" ones.

One day of loneliness may be similar, in terms of the physical stress,
as smoking a whole pack of cigarettes.[8] Ben Sasse notes, "Persistent
loneliness reduces average longevity by more than twice as much as
heavy drinking and more than three times as much as obesity."[9] In
an age when many of the traditional social institutions are declining, the church is uniquely equipped to connect people. On average,
Christians are linked to far more people than the rest of society. As
Robert D. Putnam notes, "Regular church attendees reported talking
with 40 percent more people in the course of the day."[10]

We know a middle-aged widower who is skeptical about religion.
Still, whenever he finds himself between romantic relationships, he
feels drawn back to church. He is not seeking to spark a new romance.
Rather, his ended relationship leaves a relational void in his life, and
church seems like one of the only places that can meet that need.

When the church offers genuine community, even those who
resist the doctrine preached from the stage are still drawn to the
relationships found in the pews. We may feel the pressure to convince
people of their need for God, but we rarely have to convince them of
their need for companionship.

2. An Unstable World (Family)

Broken Families

Family is where we first learn to relate to other people, preparing us
(for good or for bad) to navigate social relationships throughout our

lives. We (the authors) are fortunate to come from a family we deeply love, but that does not mean we were free from conflicts growing up.†
Many people are less fortunate, carrying tremendous emotional baggage from broken or abusive families.

Statistically, America has one of the highest divorce rates in the world (35 to 50 percent of first marriages)[11] and 21 percent of American children are being raised without fathers.[12] The family, the foundational community unit, has been stretched and cracked, fostering lifelong hurts and distrust rather than a safe sanctuary. Today, many in the younger generation are postponing marriage—or forgoing it altogether.[13]

There has been an enlightening trend in Hollywood reflecting this. Surveying the last twenty Hollywood films we've seen, only *three* did not have a central theme of fatherhood or motherhood (or family in general). Even Disney princesses, once relegated to the quest of obtaining true love's kiss, now—in breakout films like *Frozen*—focus more on strengthening family ties than seeking charming princes. Cinema often captures the spirit of the age, and the stories emerging from Hollywood reflect a deep longing for family.

Filling in the Gaps

The Christian community is designed to fill in the gaps of our family trees. The New Testament frequently describes the Christian life in terms of family: "born again" (John 3:1–8), "adoption" (Gal. 4:5–7), and "children of God" (1 John 3:2). God is referred to as "our father"

---

† There is a patched-up hole in the wall of our childhood home that will forever stand as a memorial to one of our epic brotherly brawls. Though Mike would disagree, it is generally accepted that the match ended in a draw.

(Matt. 6:9). Paul frequently refers to fellow believers in paternal (Phil. 2:22) or sibling language (Phil. 2:25) and encourages others to treat church members as family (1 Tim. 5:1–2).

In a Heart Culture that longs for the increasingly elusive community of a loving family, the Christian church has a calling to fill that role.

Daniel's wife, Sarah, lost her father at a young age. Although she attended church sporadically, it was not until she was a teenager and attended on Father's Day that things clicked for her. As the pastor preached on God as a "father to the fatherless" (Ps. 68:5), she realized there was an answer to her longing and a balm for her loss.

Sarah is a notoriously literal person.[‡] Many of the teachings she had heard in church before had seemed too farfetched for her rational mind. This sermon proved different because it addressed one of her deepest needs. Although her current faith is built on a broad theological foundation, her entry point was the acceptance and belonging that came from a church community.

3. A Diverse and Divided World (Diversity)

Still Haven't Found What We're Looking For

Diversity is another important value in a Heart Culture. Due to technology, those growing up in the digital world are global in their perception of community and desire more diversity and inclusiveness.

Diversity is not only about a new perception but is also reflective of a new reality. The emerging generations in America are the most

---

‡ She once saw a billboard at a restaurant advertising "15 meals for under $5" and declared, "That's a great deal, but I don't know how anyone could eat 15 meals."

racially diverse in history, with multiracial children the fastest-growing demographic category.[14] Despite this new social reality, our culture frequently promotes diversity in a way that divides rather than unites.

The incongruity of events like the Oscars that attempt to champion diversity is that almost all in attendance live within a small geographical radius of each other, work in the same industry, and vote for the same political party. The speeches call for diversity, but there is no diversity in the speeches themselves—and any attempt to go off script may mean the death of the speaker's career. (Of course, Hollywood is far from the only group guilty of this behavior.) The same Heart Culture that promotes "diversity" as a central value also fosters the tribalism that deters it. We want the ideal of diversity but can't figure out how to achieve it without becoming polarized.

A prominent example is the increased importance of politics in the daily lives of many people. This is likely an attempt to fill the void of community. While it offers a version of belonging, it frequently comes at the expense of diversity. Ezra Klein observes, "We became more consistent in the party we vote for not because we came to like our party more—indeed, we've come to like the parties we vote for *less*—but because we came to dislike the opposing party more."[15]

Similarly, former Senator Ben Sasse notes that today's politics "inevitably distorts our political foes like a gigantic funhouse mirror. But we're not fully aware of this contemptuous misshaping of our fellow Americans, partly because the contortion has a calming effect on our lonely souls."[16]

Political tribalism becomes an unhealthy way for us to fulfill our longing for community. Even as people draw more and more into an isolated bubble of like-minded people, we find ourselves unhappy and in despair about the polarized state of the world. Even the LGBTQ+ alliance has demonstrated cracks in their solidarity—growing more tenuous with each added letter—as fundamental ideological differences are revealed.

Unified Diversity

Thankfully, diversity is not just a Hollywood ideal, it is a beautiful reality built into the Christian faith. J. D. Grear notes that, "Christianity is the most diverse, culturally versatile faith on the planet."[17] In contrast to the divisiveness in the culture, a church community (done correctly) knocks down barriers and promises "unified diversity" where people find connection beyond their differences.

When Jesus cleansed the temple, rebuking those who had made it a den of thieves, he quoted from Isaiah: "My house will be called a house of prayer *for all nations*" (Mark 11:17). While removing corruption from the place of worship, Christ also elevated its diversity and inclusivity.

The apostle Paul emphasized unity in the church this way: "I therefore, a prisoner for the Lord, urge you to walk in a manner worthy of the calling to which you have been called, with all humility and gentleness, with patience, bearing with one another in love, eager to maintain the unity of the Spirit in the bond of peace" (Eph. 4:1–3 ESV).

The church—as a beautifully diverse community unified in Christ—is everything the Heart Culture yearns for. But an oasis is a blessing only to those who discover and experience it. The infighting among our Christian communities is a toxin that repels a Heart Culture. We must consider the collateral damage from our circular firing squads.

In a polarized "us vs. them" world, the church must offer more than another fighter in the conflict. The Heart Culture doesn't need us to mirror their own dysfunction; they need to see a loving family unified in Jesus Christ. In a time of heightened emotion and division, the church can display a radically different vision for community.

A church that speaks effectively to a Heart Culture will be a church diverse in deed as well as in word. The church must do more than declare that it is "nonjudgmental" or "welcoming to all" or "not racist." The Heart Culture will not *feel* these truths until they *see* them on display among us.

Daniel's church intentionally displays diversity onstage. They use the announcements or Scripture readings as opportunities to celebrate the diverse ethnic, gender, and age demographics in their community. They also host events where members share traditional foods from their native cultures. Such things celebrate the diversity within the community while also strengthening the bonds and unity that connect them.

Although the children participate in the service with the adults every week, Mike's church makes one Sunday per month a child-centric service. Rather than shuffle the kids off to a distant corner of the building, it establishes (for both children and adults) that church is for all ages. When Jesus encountered children in the Gospels, He used them to teach the *adults* something. Are we so concerned about teaching the kids that we never have opportunities to learn from them?

Heaven will be the most diverse community ever assembled. If we are to point a Heart Culture toward that reality, we can start by reflecting its beauty here on earth.

4. A Broken World (Justice)

A Legacy of Justice

One reason people seek community in political tribes is to be part of social change. Although some people may associate social justice with rioting, the desire to pursue justice is often birthed from a place of deep concern. Generation Z sets high value on justice, specifically when it comes to race.[18] How to best achieve justice is a continuing conversation, but a concern for justice emerges in a Heart Culture as activism and urging companies to champion various social causes.

The Heart Culture needs to know that Jesus and His church care about justice. Jesus said, "Whatever you did for one of the least of these brothers and sisters of mine, you did for me" (Matt. 25:40). Aiding the oppressed and striving for justice are part of the Christian mission—ways we love both God and people. Citizens of the Heart Culture often want the groups they are part of to share their concern for justice, and (despite what certain cultural narratives may say) the church has historically been at the forefront of positive social change.

Christians spearheaded the abolition of the slave trade, founded universities, established orphanages, and built hospitals. The Christian worldview inspired almost every major aspect of Western society that we value today. As historian Tom Holland notes, "To live in a Western country is to live in a society still utterly saturated by Christian concepts and assumptions.... The West, increasingly empty though the pews may be, remains firmly moored to its Christian past."[19]

Today, Christians are more than twice as likely to adopt a child than the regular population is.[20] Robert D. Putnam and David E. Campbell discovered that religious people hold disproportionately higher empathy and altruism values, leading to a much higher percentage of giving and volunteering (both to religious causes inside the church and nonreligious causes outside the church).[21] In fact, research shows that even if you are not a religious person yourself, you will become a better neighbor just by spending time with people who *are* religious.[22]

A Force for Good

Despite a legacy of fighting for justice, the church today is often perceived by a Heart Culture as disengaged from the practical needs of society, gathering only to serve their own interests, and occasionally pushing back *against* the progress of society. In response to social unrest and racial division, which led to widespread riots and tension, many preachers declared, "It's not a skin problem; it's a sin problem!" It affirmed the narrative that the church is only concerned about spiritual matters disconnected from their physical manifestations, what Hans R. Rookmaaker calls, "a ghost-like spirituality without a body."[23]

There is a danger in allowing social causes to overshadow other aspects of our Christian identity and purpose. Nevertheless, the church was always meant to be a force for good in the world, as "salt and light" that counteracts the decay and darkness around us (Matt. 5:13–16). A Heart Culture's passion for justice opens them up to the vision of community displayed through Jesus in the kingdom of God.

The church should offer a transcendent experience of worship that is not found anywhere else in the culture. But this relationship to God must also manifest itself in practical love for others. A Heart Culture wants to put their passions into action, and if such opportunities are not available within the Christian community, they will seek other communities.

Those who are not yet part of our church communities don't see the worship that takes place in our Sunday gatherings. They are not part of our Bible studies, youth groups, and Wednesday night dinners. What they *do* see is the action we take in the wider society. What will they come to understand about our church communities from the observable way we put our love into practice?

5. A Digital World (Presence)

Community through a Screen

When the COVID-19 pandemic confined people to their homes, online video platforms such as Zoom suddenly went from a daily global usage peak of ten million to more than two hundred million.[24] People were desperate to find community, even if it came through a screen.

Many churches that had been slow or reluctant to adopt digital components to their gatherings were suddenly forced to invest in video equipment and offer livestreams. Protestant churches that livestreamed all or part of their worship service jumped from 27 percent to 97 percent.[25] Christians saw the immense benefits of digital tools to keep communities connected but were also left with many unanswered questions as to what kind of community they were fostering.

If a Heart Culture is increasingly online, then the church cannot shrink away from digital spaces. At the same time, just because we meet people there doesn't mean we leave them there. Imagine you have a lonely and depressed friend who hunkers down in his basement watching sad movies for months after a painful breakup. As his friend, you could deliver some "positive" comedy movies to his doorstep, making his self-imposed isolation more tolerable. However, what he likely needs is an invitation to come outside into the sun, take a hike in God's creation, and laugh with someone rather than continue in digital isolation.

Nearly 25 percent of Millennials and Gen Z, the world's first digital natives, are now being treated for depression.[26] Technology is not the only factor, but we must not overlook the fact that society is more digital than ever and those most immersed in that technology are as depressed as ever. Psychologist Jonathan Haidt has studied the disturbing climb in teen depression, anxiety, and self-harm (especially among girls), and he believes that it correlates with increased social media usage, as the younger generation went from a *play-based childhood* to a *phone-based childhood*.[27]

The "social" aspect of social media has not necessarily given us better relationships, even if it has given us more widespread connections. As churches scramble to follow people into digital spaces, we should discern whether we are doing so merely to keep up with social trends, or if we are truly driven to foster healthy communities.

Countercultural Presence

Much of the New Testament comprises letters written by Paul to Christian communities with whom he could not at that moment be physically present. Technology and social media can be an extension of this approach. Robert D. Putnam offers the term "alloys" when addressing the question of "technology or real relationships."[28] Just as an alloy is created when two separate metals come together, in-person and online relationships can form something new that takes on aspects of each.

Technology can connect people across distances. Our mother has a digital community of women she calls her "committee." Long ago, they were all youth group friends together, but now they live scattered across North America. Every morning, they make coffee, get online at the scheduled time, and fellowship. They don't even use video (this is pre-coffee o'clock in the morning, after all); they just text. The community has been no less real, no less edifying, despite having not been face-to-face for decades.

On the other hand, Sherry Turkle observes that in our new reality, "Virtual places offer connection with uncertain claims to commitment."[29] As a result of this ambiguous belonging and lack of accountability, we are confused about when we are "alone" and when we are "together."[30] A person may identify with a certain church or other digital community after watching their livestreams for months, but when a crisis strikes the person's home, she suddenly finds herself alone and anonymous. Research is finding that online social connections can contribute to overall well-being *if* they lead to in-person connections and don't remain exclusively online.[310]

Have you ever listened to a "live" album by a band? They're great for people who live in places where the band would never tour (like Daniel, who lives in the southern United States and yet is a self-proclaimed connoisseur of European power metal). Still, great as live recordings are, nobody claims to have been to a concert after listening to such an album, no matter how much crowd noise the producers leave in the mix. They are both good experiences, but they are *different*.

Technology offers a tremendous opportunity for the church to intersect with the lives of people, but a virtual world cannot fully substitute for what we gain by physically meeting in pairs, small groups, or large gatherings.

Within a Heart Culture longing for genuine connectivity, the church can provide a sense of "presence." As the church, we have an opportunity to use online tools, but we must use them wisely so they will ultimately lead to in-person connections. In a rapidly digitizing world, perhaps what people need most from the church is not for our communities to just offer more disembodied content, but to be countercultural in preserving the beauty of face-to-face community.

Conclusion

Mary Shelley's *Frankenstein* is widely considered the first science fiction story ever written. In the book, the iconic creature does not begin as the horrific killing machine we know it as today. The inhuman

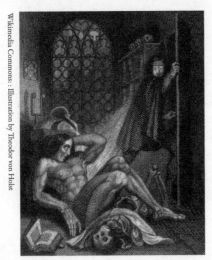

scientific creation of Dr. Victor Frankenstein begins as an innocent creature searching for love and connection. But when society rejects him and his creator refuses to create a mate for companionship, the creature mourns: "I am alone, and miserable; man will not associate with me."[32] From that moment, the creature becomes increasingly violent and detached, lashing out from the pain of its own loneliness and ultimately becoming a monster.

Illustration from Mary Shelley's *Frankenstein*

Wikimedia Commons: Illustration by Theodor von Holst

Isolation is dehumanizing because it goes against our nature. As a trinitarian Being, God exists in eternal relationship. As creatures made in His image, we share that fundamental desire to live alongside others. Fellowship is not table dressing for more important concerns; it is a necessity if we are to experience the abundant life God offers.

On the front page of the American Atheists' website is the statement: "Millions of people who no longer believe stay in their churches because of the community and support the churches provide. Our local affiliates stand ready to help and are vibrant communities full of people just like you who have left behind religion."[33] People are driven toward community; the only question is where they will find it.

Many have left the church because their hearts were broken by the people inside. Others already on the outside see the dysfunction in the church and feel compelled to find fellowship elsewhere. In a digital and divided world that is becoming increasingly lonely, depressed, and disconnected, we must live up to our calling.

The Heart Culture yearns for community. Rather than reflect the same divisive, exclusive, and tribal spirit of the age, we can be a way station for weary travelers to warm themselves by the fire and find fellowship.

Conclusion

Christianity is, in the long run and deep down, reasonable, but it is
certainly not "reasonable" in the short run or in the obvious appearances.
It is not an obvious or easy thing to believe.

—Peter Kreeft

The human mind can be pragmatic because deep down it is romantic.

—David Brooks

An Unexpected Plot Twist

One of our favorite films is *Signs* (2002), a science fiction/horror film
by director M. Night Shyamalan. The film centers on Graham Hess, a
former priest who has become broken and disillusioned with the world
following the tragic death of his wife. (Also, aliens! But we'll get to
them in a second.)

Throughout the movie, Graham's young daughter has the habit of
leaving water glasses unfinished, to the frustration of her father. These
half-empty glasses scattered throughout the house are visible in many
scenes. They are a trivial annoyance, but on a deeper level, they act as a
symbol for Graham losing control of his surroundings—a single parent who cannot maintain a clean house or understand his daughter.
They are a sign that represents how his life has spiraled out of control
and how he yearns to return to the past when things were different.

The movie is science fiction, so eventually a more pressing challenge emerges in the form of aliens invading earth. Taking place almost exclusively in the farmhouse, the movie expertly builds tension as Graham struggles to protect his family. As a storyteller, Shyamalan is synonymous with "plot twists," and he lives up to his reputation. (Warning: spoilers ahead.)

As the situation becomes increasingly dire, the characters inadvertently discover that these extraterrestrial invaders have one crippling weakness: their bodies cannot tolerate water. As Graham stands in the living room facing down the alien that has taken his son hostage, he sees the unfinished water glasses all around him. What he had become accustomed to seeing as a problem is now viewed as a hopeful solution and the means to his family's salvation.

Eyes Open to a New Perspective

We live in a Heart Culture. Everywhere we look, we see reminders. Each shocking headline, societal outcry, or sobering statistic about the declining relevance of the church is an uncomfortable sign that reinforces our feeling that the world is spiraling out of control.

The question we have been exploring throughout the book is this: What if the very aspects of the culture that fill us with foreboding are also the unexpected solution to the problem? What if the beating pulse of the culture is not a droning gong that leaves our heads throbbing but is rather a summons to our hearts? In short: What if the Heart Culture is not a problem but a possibility?

We are under no delusions that you have agreed with us on every point along our journey together. The heart is a mystifying place, and the highways running in and out of it are rarely straight or clearly marked. Our objective has not been to provide a step-by-step cultural engagement manual. Rather, as in H. G. Wells's story *The Country of the Blind*, our hope is to have opened your eyes to exciting new possibilities the Heart Culture presents for our Christian mission.

We are thankful for the herculean efforts and rational approach of Christian intellectuals and apologists. It was through their writing that we developed our critical thinking skills and gained confidence in the rational foundations of our childhood faith. If humans are unavoidably beings of *both* head and heart, then those who eloquently speak the language of the head will always have a role in the Christian mission. But we must all be bilingual. To effectively engage with the world today, we must also speak the language of the heart.

God is not contrary to reason, but
He is certainly *beyond* reason.

In a Head Culture, rational apologetics and cultural engagement were developed largely as an antidote to an illness caused *by* the rational mind. The Head Culture was a place where the logical head demystified and rationalized away the supernatural realities of the world. The culture was rejecting divine creation in favor of random chance, excusing the miraculous as hallucinations, and providing a megaphone for the New Atheists to call many Christians off the path of faith.

Simply returning to a Head Culture is not the solution to what ails the world today. A rational approach to apologetics read the culture and responded appropriately and effectively to the questions they were asking. But now, as the questions within culture change, we must allow our approach to adapt.

Until Christ's triumphant return, both a Head Culture and a Heart Culture will inevitably provide fertile soil for missional engagement. Humans are a union of the two. As the church, let us be less concerned with trying to force the culture into the paradigm of our choosing and instead be more driven to engage effectively with the people who surround us. Whether that calls for an appeal to the head or the heart, our mission remains unchanged: to help guide hungry and thirsty people to the banquet table of Jesus Christ.

It All Starts with the Heart

The heart language is not a trendy new invention. We find it throughout Scripture. Peter Kreeft observes, "The Bible is mercilessly silent about arguments to persuade the hopeless fool who says there is no God, but it continually reassures us that God is not immoral or amoral but good and trustable, and is working out all things for an eventually stunning consummation of beauty and justice and joy for all who dare to love him and trust him."[1]

Notice how the apostle Paul instructs the church in Colossae:

> My goal is that they may be encouraged in *heart* and
> united in *love*, so that they may have the full riches
> of complete understanding, in order that they may
> know the mystery of God, namely, Christ, in whom
> are hidden all the treasures of *wisdom* and *knowledge*.
> I tell you this so that no one may deceive you by fine-
> sounding arguments. (Col. 2:2–4)

To counter persuasive arguments and misleading ideologies, Paul did not provide a detailed list of equally rational counterpoints. Instead, he appealed to the heart and to the enticing "mystery" of the faith. If their *hearts* came to grasp the truth of Christ, their heads would eventually be blessed by "wisdom and knowledge." The two are vitally connected, and the head is downstream of the heart.

The Christian faith is not an easy thing to believe, nor should we expect it to be. A God who could be wholly conceived within the finite human mind would be a small deity indeed. There is nothing immediately rational about the doctrine of the trinity, or the hypostatic union of Jesus, or eternity, or miracles, or the omnipresence of an invisible Being. Paul speaks truly when he confesses that the Christian gospel is "foolishness to those who are perishing, but to us who are being saved it is the power of God" (1 Cor. 1:18).

God is not contrary to reason, but He is certainly *beyond* reason. Or perhaps it is better to say that He is beyond what we might *call* reasonable from our limited perspective. We don't embrace divine truths because they fit nicely into our logical understanding. Rather, we accept them by faith because the experiential knowledge of God (perceived by our hearts) opens our spiritual eyes to the reality of more than what is obvious to our rational minds. We embrace those bewildering mysteries of God because somehow they confirm what we know in our hearts to be true.

One of the most honest statements in the entire Bible is, "I do believe; help me overcome my unbelief!" (Mark 9:24b). Our hearts often perceive the truth first through what we experience, and our heads must catch up. A heart approach does not work in opposition to the head but in harmony with it, expanding the possibilities of reason and cultivating an appetite for that which goes beyond a strictly logical understanding.

Speaking the Heart Language

In this book, we have explored five "dialects" of the heart language, different pathways to communicate the reality of our faith straight to the heart of the culture. To review:

Story: As people wired for narrative, we can speak through the stories we live, the stories we tell, and the stories others are telling all around us.

Beauty: In an increasingly industrialized world, we can point people to "pockets of beauty" that show the attractiveness of God.

Art: In a culture immersed in and shaped by the arts, we can cultivate and encourage creativity in the church, then send artists out as cultural missionaries.

Desire: In a passionate world driven by deep desires of love, identity, purpose, and transcendence, we can show how Jesus is the perfect fulfillment of each.

Community: As relational creatures in a world of disappearing social connectivity, the church can offer a community of unified diversity.

The nature of any language is that it is living, constantly in flux, always expanding and changing. These five areas are not meant to be exhaustive but are simply possible applications of communicating to the heart. How will we learn to speak this new language most effectively? The way we learn any language: by listening.

As news headlines splash across your screen and political posts flood your social media feed—or people in your church, community, and family make seemingly incomprehensible decisions—resist the urge to react out of frustration. Instead, open your ears to what others are communicating so you can respond appropriately. Remember that these are not the violent shouts of an enemy but the voice of a restless culture crying for help in the language of their hearts.

A People for a Language

J. R. R. Tolkien is most famous as the author of *The Lord of the Rings*, but his primary vocation was as a philologist (someone who studies the history of languages). He developed his cherished fantasy tales as an outflow of his interest in languages, rather than the other way around. He did not invent "elvish" because he needed a language for his story; he wrote a story because he needed a history for his invented language. Tolkien understood the synergy between a people and their language. To understand a language, you must understand its people.

A language is not just how we communicate but an outworking of who we are. Heart language can communicate the Christian faith effectively because it is consistent with the nature of how God created us. It ultimately points back to *His* heart, because we are created in His image (Gen. 1:27). We can speak and understand heart language because, deep down, we are heart people. The heart language is not just a tool we use to speak to the world, but it is also a vehicle through which we can come to understand ourselves.

Leo Tolstoy's classic novel *Anna Karenina* is regularly voted among the greatest works of literature. It tells the sprawling tale of interconnected characters as they strive to obtain a satisfying life. One of the most captivating characters is Konstantin Levin. He has achieved an outwardly good life, and yet he remains a tortured character, miserable to the point of contemplating suicide. While the other characters follow the inflamed passion of their hearts into misery, Levin is the exception. He is supremely rational, navigating the world with his head rather than his heart, but for all that, he is unable to diagnose the cause of his discontent.

Finally, at the end of the novel, after a seemingly insignificant encounter with a humble peasant, he has an epiphany: "To my heart has been revealed a knowledge beyond all doubt, and unattainable by reason, and here I am obstinately trying to express that knowledge in

Illustration of Kevin and Kitty from *Anna Karenina*

reason and words."[2] Some realities of life and happiness could not be gleaned secondhand through his rational mind but could come only by opening his heart to their experience—inexplicable as they may seem. The novel concludes with these words:

> My reason will still not understand why I pray, but I shall still pray, and my life, my whole life, independently of anything that may happen to me, is every moment of it no longer meaningless as it was before, but has an unquestionable meaning of goodness with which I have the power to invest it.[3]

In that enlightening moment, although Levin's rational head had not made sense of all the confounding mysteries of life, in his heart he had finally caught a waft of the alluring scent of the heavenly banquet table.

As Christians, we cannot lead a hungry and restless culture somewhere we have not been ourselves. Our final prayer for you is that this book has opened your heart up to new ways to taste and experience the goodness of God (Ps. 34:8). That, in coming before God with "all your heart and with all your soul and with all your mind" (Mark 12:30), you will be utterly and completely enveloped by and infused with the irresistible smell of the banquet feast. That everywhere you go, all who cross your path will be drawn closer to the person of Jesus Christ, the One who can satisfy the deepest yearnings of their hearts.

Recommended Reading List

Crouch, Andy. *Culture Making: Recovering Our Creative Calling.* Downers Grove, IL: IVP Books, 2008.

Fujimura. Makoto. *Culture Care: Reconnecting with Beauty for Our Common Life.* Downers Grove, IL: IVP Books, 2017.

Hildebrand, Dietrich von. *Aesthetics,* vol. 1. Steubenville, OH: Hildebrand Project, 2016.

Hildebrand, Dietrich von. *Beauty in the Light of Redemption.* Steubenville, OH: Hildebrand Press, 2019.

Kahneman, Daniel. *Thinking, Fast and Slow.* Toronto: Anchor Canada, 2013.

Kreeft, Peter. *The Wisdom of the Heart: The Good, the True, and the Beautiful at the Center of Us All.* Gastonia, NC: TAN Books, 2020.

McManus, Erwin Raphael. *The Artisan Soul: Crafting Your Life into a Work of Art.* New York: HarperOne, 2014.

Prior, Karen Swallow. *On Reading Well: Finding the Good Life through Great Books.* Grand Rapids, MI: Brazos Press, 2018.

Putnam, Robert D. *Bowling Alone: The Collapse and Revival of American Community.* New York: Simon & Schuster, 2020.

Schaeffer, Francis A. *Art and the Bible.* Downers Grove, IL: IVP Books, 1973.

Sire, James. *Apologetics Beyond Reason.* Downers Grove, IL: IVP Academic, 2014.

Smith, James K. A. *You Are What You Love.* Grand Rapids, MI: Brazos Press, 2016.

Trueman, Carl R. *The Rise and Triumph of the Modern Self: Cultural Amnesia, Expressive Individualism, and the Road to Sexual Revolution.* Wheaton, IL: Crossway, 2020.

Trueman, Carl R. *Strange New World: How Thinkers and Activists Redefined Identity and Sparked the Sexual Revolution.* Wheaton, IL: Crossway, 2022.

Turner, Steve. *Imagine: A Vision for Christians in the Arts,* revised and expanded. Downers Grove, IL: IVP Books, 2017.

Notes

Introduction

1. David Kinnaman, *You Lost Me: Why Young Christians Are Leaving the Church,* (Grand Rapids, MI: Baker Books, 2011), 38.

2. J. R. R. Tolkien, *The Lord of the Rings Illustrated* (New York: William Morrow, 2021), 880.

3. Carl Trueman, *The Rise and Triumph of the Modern Self: Cultural Amnesia, Expressive Individualism, and the Road to Sexual Revolution* (Wheaton, IL: Crossway, 2020), 30.

4. Gary Chapman, *The Five Love Languages: The Secret to Love That Lasts* (Chicago: Northfield, 1992).

Chapter 1: A Culture That Lost Its Mind (but Found Its Heart)

1. Mark Twain, *Following the Equator: A Journey around the World* (New York: Doubleday & McClure, 1897), 156.

2. Lewis Carroll, *Alice's Adventures in Wonderland & Through the Looking-Glass and What Alice Found There* (London: Oxford University Press, 1971), 177.

3. H. G. Wells, *The Country of the Blind* (London: Golden Cockerel Press, 1939), 30.

4. Sam Harris, *The End of Faith: Religion, Terror, and the Future of Reason* (New York: W. W. Norton, 2004), 16.

5. Sam Harris, *Letter to a Christian Nation* (New York: Vintage Books, 2008), 67.

6. Rodney Stark, *The Rise of Christianity: How the Obscure, Marginal Jesus Movement Became the Dominant Religious Force in the Western World in a Few Centuries* (New York: HarperOne, 1996), 37.

7. Alister McGrath, *Why God Won't Go Away* (Nashville: Thomas Nelson, 2010), 87.

8. Valerie Richardson, "Leigh Finke, Transgender Legislator, Wins USA Today 2023 'Women of the Year' Honors," *Washington Times*, March 21, 2023, www.washingtontimes.com/news/2023/mar/21/leigh-finke-transgender -legislator-wins-usa-today-.

9. *Dead Poets Society*, directed by Peter Weir (1989; United States: Buena Vista Pictures Distribution, 1998), DVD.

10. Thomas Nagel, *The Last Word* (New York: Oxford University Press, 1997), 130.

11. Aaron Earls, "Most Teenagers Drop Out of Church When They Become Young Adults," Lifeway Research, January 15, 2019, https://research.lifeway.com/2019 /01/15/most-teenagers-drop-out-of-church-as-young-adults/.

12. David Kinnaman, *You Lost Me: Why Young Christians Are Leaving the Church* (Grand Rapids, MI: Baker Books, 2011), 92–93.

13. Kinnaman, 67.

Chapter 2: The Rational Irrationality of Heart People

1. *Space Jam*, directed by Joe Pytka (1996; Warner Bros. Family Entertainment).

2. Jonathan Haidt, *The Righteous Mind: Why Good People Are Divided by Politics and Religion* (New York: Vintage Books, 2012), 32.

3. J. K. Rowling, *Harry Potter and the Order of the Phoenix* (New York: Scholastic, 2003), 459.

4. Dante Alighieri, *Convivio*, ed. and trans. Andrew Frisardi (Cambridge, UK: Cambridge University Press, 2017), 161.

5. Haidt, *The Righteous Mind*, 47.

6. David Kahneman, *Thinking, Fast and Slow* (Toronto: Anchor Canada, 2013), 81.

7. Adam Grant, *Think Again: The Power of Knowing What You Don't Know* (New York: Viking, 2021), 24.

8. Brian Regan, *Brian Regan: On the Rocks*, dir. Troy Miller, Netflix, 2023.

9. Haidt, *The Righteous Mind*, 50–51.

10. David Brooks, *The Social Animal: The Hidden Sources of Love, Character, and Achievement* (New York: Random House, 2012), 21.

11. Charles Dickens, *Hard Times* (London: J. M. Dent & Sons, 1908), 1.

12. Maddy Shaw Roberts, "I Played the Shark Theme to Spielberg and He Said, 'You Can't Be Serious!' – John Williams on Composing Jaws," Classic FM, August 29, 2022, www.classicfm.com/composers/williams/jaws-theme-spielberg-joke/.

13. Kathryn Kalinak, *Film Music: A Very Short Introduction* (Oxford: Oxford University Press, 2010), 18–19.

Chapter 3: Straight to the Heart

1. Neal Gabler, *An Empire of Their Own: How the Jews Invented Hollywood* (New York: Anchor Books, 1989), 6–7.

2. Gabler, 432.

3. Andrew Fletcher, *An Account of a Conversation Concerning a Right Regulation of Governments for the Common Good of Mankind* (Edinburgh: Oxford University, 1704), 10.

4. Peter Kreeft, *Wisdom of the Heart: The Good, the True, and the Beautiful at the Center of Us All* (Gastonia, NC: TAN Books, 2020), 289.

5. Philip Graham Ryken, *Art for God's Sake: A Call to Recover the Arts* (Phillipsburg, NJ: P & R, 2006), 33.

6. Leland Ryken, "'I Have Used Similitudes': The Poetry of the Bible," *Bibliotheca Sacra* 147 (July 1990): 259.

7. Gordon D. Fee and Douglas Stuart, *How to Read the Bible for All Its Worth,* 4th ed. (Grand Rapids, MI: Zondervan, 2014), 93.

8. Rebecca McLaughlin, *Confronting Christianity: 12 Hard Questions for the World's Largest Religion* (Wheaton, IL: Crossway, 2019), 135.

9. Lawlor, H. J., "St. Paul's Quotations from Epimenides," *The Irish Church Quarterly*, vol. 9. No. 35. (Jul. 1916), 180-193, p 180.

10. Eratosthenes, Hyginus, and Aratus, *Constellation Myths with Aratus's Phaenomena,* trans. Robin Hard (Oxford: Oxford University Press, 2015), 139.

11. Joseph Campbell and Bill Moyers, *The Power of Myth* (New York: Anchor, 1991), xvi.

Chapter 4: Story

1. James Sire, *The Universe Next Door*, 5th ed. (Downers Grove, IL: IVP Academic, 2009), 10.

2. Kevin Jackson, "Arts: The Man Who Was Yoda," *Independent*, September 3, 1999, www.independent.co.uk/arts-entertainment/arts-the-man-who-was-yoda -1115705.html.

3. Susan Cain, *Quiet: The Power of Introverts in a World That Can't Stop Talking* (New York: Broadway Books, 2014), 263.

4. Jonathan Haidt, *The Happiness Hypothesis: Finding Modern Truth in Ancient Wisdom* (New York: Basic Books, 2006), 147–148. Haidt draws from the research found in Jamie Pennebaker's *Opening Up*.

5. Daniel Kahneman, *Thinking, Fast and Slow* (Toronto: Anchor Canada, 2013), 381.

6. C. S. Lewis, *The Collected Letters of C. S. Lewis: Family Letters 1905–1931*, ed. Walter Hooper (New York: HarperCollins, 2004), 977.

7. Eugene Lowry, *The Homiletical Plot: The Sermon as Narrative Art Form* (Louisville, KY: Westminster John Knox Press, 2001), 12.

8. Lowry, 24.

9. Kelly Knauer and Ellen Shapiro, *TIME: The 100 Most Influential People Who Never Lived* (New York: Time Books, 2013), vi.

10. F. Scott Fitzgerald, *F. Scott Fitzgerald on Writing*, ed. Larry W. Phillips (New York: Scribner, 1986), 10.

11. Humphrey Carpenter, *J. R. R. Tolkien: A Biography* (New York: Houghton Mifflin, 1977), 151.

12. James Sire, *Apologetics beyond Reason: Why Seeing Is Really Believing* (Downers Grove, IL: IVP Academic, 2014), 48.

Chapter 5: Beauty

1. "Spanish Fresco Restoration Botched by Amateur," *BBC News*, August 23, 2012, www.bbc.com/news/world-europe-19349921.

2. Zachary Kussin, "Spanish Town Celebrates 10th Anniversary of Botched 'Ecce Homo' Fresco," *New York Post*, September 9, 2022, https://nypost.com/2022 /09/09/spanish-town-marks-anniversary-of-botched-ecce-homo-fresco/.

3. Charles Darwin, *On the Origin of Species* (New York: Barnes & Noble Classics, 2004), 384.

4. Amy Maxmen, "Come Mate with Me," *Nature*, October 7, 2015, www.nature .com/articles/526S8a.

5. Charles Darwin, *The Autobiography of Charles Darwin: 1809–1882*, ed. Nora Barlow (New York: W. W. Norton, 1958), 139.

6. Gustave Flaubert, *The Letters of Gustave Flaubert: 1830–1857*, trans. Francis Steegmuller (Cambridge, MA: Belknap Press, 1980), 158.

7. Nancy Pearcey, *Saving Leonardo: A Call to Resist the Secular Assault on Mind, Morals, and Meaning* (Nashville: B & H Books, 2010), 156.

8. Peter Kreeft, *Wisdom of the Heart: The Good, the True, and the Beautiful at the Center of Us All* (Gastonia, NC: TAN Books, 2020) 294.

9. Arthur C. Danto, *The Abuse of Beauty: Aesthetics and the Concept of Art* (Chicago: Open Court, 2003), 15.

10. John Keats, "Ode on a Grecian Urn," in *John Keats: The Complete Poems,* 3rd ed., ed. John Barnard (New York: Penguin, 1977), 346.

11. Dietrich von Hildebrand, *Aesthetics*, vol. 1 (Steubenville, OH: Hildebrand Project, 2016), 138.

12. Dietrich von Hildebrand, *Beauty in the Light of Redemption* (Steubenville, OH: Hildebrand Press, 2019), 22.

13. H. G. Wells, *The Country of the Blind* (London: Golden Cockerel Press, 1939), 45.

14. C. S. Lewis, *The Lion, the Witch and the Wardrobe* (New York: Macmillan, 1950), 123.

15. Kreeft, *Wisdom of the Heart,* 282.

16. Hildebrand, *Beauty in the Light of the Redemption*, 21.

17. J. R. R. Tolkien, *The Tolkien Reader* (New York: Del Rey, 1986), 31.

18. Jo Piazza, "Audiences Experience 'Avatar' Blues," CNN, January 11, 2010, www.cnn.com/2010/SHOWBIZ/Movies/01/11/avatar.movie.blues/index.html.

19. Francis Collins, *The Language of God: A Scientist Presents Evidence for Belief* (New York: Free Press, 2006), 35-36.

20. Steve Paulson, "The Believer," *Salon*, August 7, 2006, www.salon.com/2006/08/07/collins_6/.

21. Aaron Earls, "4 Reasons People Haven't Come Back to Church," Lifeway Research, June 7, 2023, https://research.lifeway.com/2023/06/07/4-reasons-people-havent-come-back-to-church/, accessed June 13, 2023.

22. Fyodor Dostoevsky, *The Idiot* (New York: Barnes & Noble Classics, 2005), 351.

23. Hildebrand, *Beauty in the Light of Redemption*, 5.

24. Mother Teresa, *The Joy in Loving: A Guide to Daily Living* (New York: Viking Penguin, 1997), 47.

25. J. R. R. Tolkien, *The Return of the King* (Ballantine Books: New York, 2018), 211.

Chapter 6: Art

1. "Live Auction 1514: Impressionist and Modern Art (Evening Sale), Christie's, accessed October 2, 2023, www.christies.com/en/lot/lot-4488033.

2. Oscar Wilde, "Preface," in *The Picture of Dorian Gray* (1891; repr., Mineola, NY: Dover Publications, 1993), viii.

3. Steven Pinker, *How the Mind Works* (New York: W. W. Norton, 2009), 528–534.

4. Robert D. Putnam and David E. Campbell, *American Grace: How Religion Divides and Unites Us* (New York: Simon & Schuster, 2010), 447.

5. Neil Postman, *Amusing Ourselves to Death*, 20th anniversary ed. (New York: Penguin Books, 2006), 61.

6. Dorothy L. Sayers, "Toward a Christian Aesthetic," in *Unpopular Opinions* (London: Camelot Press, 1946), 29.

7. Paul Munson and Joshua Farris Drake, *Art and Music: A Student's Guide* (Wheaton, IL: Crossway, 2014), 39.

8. Andy Crouch, *Culture Making: Recovering Our Creative Calling* (Downers Grove, IL: IVP, 2009), 67.

9. James K.A. Smith. *You Are What You Love: The Spiritual Power of Habit.* (Grand Rapids: Brazos Press, 2016), 11

10. Francis A. Schaeffer, *Art and the Bible* (Downers Grove, IL: IVP Books, 1973), 18.

11. Andrew Peterson, *The Warden and the Wolf King*, The Wingfeather Saga: Book 4 (Colorado Springs: Waterbrook, 2020), 224.

12. James MacMillan, "The Most Spiritual of the Arts: Music, Modernity, and the Search for the Sacred," in *Annunciations: Sacred Music for the Twenty-First Century*, ed. George Corbett (Cambridge, UK: Open Book, 2019), 9.

13. Mark Galli and Ted Olsen, eds., *131 Christians Everyone Should Know* (Nashville: Holman Reference, 2000), 110

NOTES 185

14. Liz Todd, "Why I Celebrate Christmas, by the World's Most Famous Atheist,"
Daily Mail, December 23, 2008, www.dailymail.co.uk/debate/article-1100842
/Why-I-celebrate-Christmas-worlds-famous-atheist.html.

15. Dietrich von Hildebrand, *Aesthetics*, vol. 1 (Steubenville, OH: Hildebrand
Project, 2016), 248–249.

16. Emily Dickinson, *The Complete Poems of Emily Dickinson*, ed. Thomas H.
Johnson (Boston: Back Bay Books, 1976), 506.

Chapter 7: Desire

1. *Hollywood, Teach Us to Pray*, documentary produced by Terry Lindvall (Cries of
the Heart, Virginia Wesleyan University, 2023).

2. Neil Gaiman, "Who Are the New Gods?" posted by American Gods, July 12,
2017, YouTube video, 1:06, www.youtube.com/watch?v=2VZGfce3wjk&t=11s.

3. C. S. Lewis, *Mere Christianity* (New York: Harper One, 1952), 136–137.

4. Augustine, *The Confessions of Saint Augustine*, trans. John K. Ryan (New York:
Image Books), 43.

5. Blaise Pascal, *Pensées* (New York: Penguin, 1196), 4.

6. *Cinderella*, directed by Clyde Geronimi, Wilfred Jackson, and Hamilton Luske
(1950; Walt Disney Animation Studios).

7. Michelle Lee-Barnewall, *Neither Complementarian nor Egalitarian: A Kingdom
Corrective to the Evangelical Gender Debate* (Grand Rapids, MI: Baker Academic,
2016), 161.

8. James K. A. Smith, *You Are What You Love* (Grand Rapids, MI: Brazos Press,
2016), 10.

9. Tony Reinke, *Competing Spectacles: Treasuring Christ in the Media Age*
(Wheaton, IL: Crossway, 2019), 66.

10. James Clear, *Atomic Habits: An Easy & Proven Way to Build Good Habits &
Break Bad Ones* (New York: Avery, 2018), 108.

11. David Brooks, "Building Better Secularists," *New York Times*, February 3, 2015,
www.nytimes.com/2015/02/03/opinion/david-brooks-building-better-secularists
.html.

12. C. S. Lewis, "Afterword to Third Edition," in *The Pilgrim's Regress* (Grand
Rapids, MI: William B. Eerdmans, 2014), 237.

13. See Alvin Plantinga, "Reason and Belief in God," in *Faith and Rationality: Reason and Belief in God*, eds. Alvin Plantinga and Nicholas Wolterstorff (Notre Dame: University of Notre Dame Press, 1983).

14. Rudolf Otto, *The Idea of the Holy: An Inquiry into the Non-Rational Factor in the Idea of the Divine and Its Relation to the Rational*, trans. John W. Harvey (London: Oxford University Press, 1924), 13.

15. Antoine de Saint-Exupery, *The Wisdom of the Sands* (New York: Harcourt Brace, 1950).

Chapter 8: Community

1. Jonathan Haidt, *The Happiness Hypothesis: Finding Modern Truth in Ancient Wisdom* (New York: Basic Books, 2006), 134.

2. Dan Witters, "U.S. Depression Rates Reach New Highs," Gallup, May 17, 2023, https://news.gallup.com/poll/505745/depression-rates-reach-new-highs.aspx. William A. Haseltine, "Young People Hit Hardest by Loneliness and Depression During Covid-19," *Forbes*, April 13, 2021, www.forbes.com/sites/williamhaseltine /2021/04/13/young-people-hit-hardest-by-loneliness-and-depression-during-covid -19/?sh=57ae5b7d5f0b.

3. David Kinnaman and Mark Matlock, *Faith for Exiles: 5 Ways for a New Generation to Follow Jesus in Digital Babylon* (Grand Rapids, MI: Baker Books, 2019), 115.

4. Jefferson Bethke, "Why I Hate Religion, but Love Jesus: Spoken Word," posted by Jeff & Alyssa, January 10, 2012, YouTube video, 4:03, www.youtube.com/watch ?v=1IAhDGYlpqY.

5. "Meet Those Who Love Jesus but Not the Church," Barna, March 30, 2017, www.barna.com/research/meet-love-jesus-not-church/.

6. Rodney Stark, *Discovering God: The Origins of the Great Religions and the Evolution of Belief* (New York: HarperOne, 2007), 311.

7. You can read his entire report here: www.hhs.gov/sites/default/files/surgeon -general-social-connection-advisory.pdf.

8. Ben Sasse, *Them: Why We Hate Each Other—And How to Heal* (New York: St. Martin's Press, 2018), 22.

9. Sasse, 23.

10. Robert D. Putnam, *Bowling Alone: The Collapse and Revival of American Community* (New York: Simon & Schuster, 2000), 67.

11. "Divorce Rate by State," World Population Review, updated January 2023, https://worldpopulationreview.com/state-rankings/divorce-rate-by-state, accessed June 1, 2023.

12. Paul Hemez and Chanell Washington, "Percentage and Number of Children Living with Two Parents Has Dropped Since 1968," US Census Bureau, April 12, 2021, www.census.gov/library/stories/2021/04/number-of-children-living-only-with-their-mothers-has-doubled-in-past-50-years.html.

13. Ari Blaff, "U.S. Marriage Rate Has Declined 60 Percent Since 1970, Study Shows," *National Review*, February 25, 2023, www.nationalreview.com/news /u-s-marriage-rate-has-declined-60-percent-since-1970-study-shows/.

14. James Emery White, *Meet Generation Z: Understanding and Reaching the New Post-Christian World* (Grand Rapids, MI: Baker Books, 2017), 46.

15. Ezra Klein, *Why We're Polarized* (New York: Avid Reader Press, 2020), 10.

16. Sasse, *Them: Why We Hate Each Other—And How to Heal*, 80-81.

17. J. D. Greear, "Does Diversity in the Church Even Matter?," J. D. Greear Ministries, December 15, 2014, https://jdgreear.com/does-diversity-in-the-church -even-matter/.

18. "How the Church Can Fuel Black Gen Z's Desire for Justice," Barna, February 22, 2023, www.barna.com/research/black-gen-z-justice/.

19. Tom Holland, *Dominion: The Making of the Western World* (London: Abacus, 2020), xxv.

20. "5 Things You Need to Know about Adoption," Barna, November 4, 2013, www.barna.com/research/5-things-you-need-to-know-about-adoption /#.UnvPco2E7Tw.

21. Robert D. Putnam and David E. Campbell, *American Grace: How Religion Divides and Unites Us* (New York: Simon & Schuster, 2010), 446, 464.

22. Putnam and Campbell, 475.

23. Hans R. Rookmaaker, *Art Needs No Justification* (Vancouver, BC: Regent College, 1978), 21.

24. "Zoom Pulls in More Than 200 Million Daily Video Users during Worldwide Lockdowns," Reuters, April 2, 2020, www.reuters.com/article/us-health-coronavirus -zoom-idUSKBN21K1C7.

25. Aaron Earls, "Online Services Expanded Reach of Churches During Pandemic," Lifeway Research, October 14, 2021, https://research.lifeway.com/2021/10/14/online-services-expanded-reach-of-churches-during-pandemic/.

26. Dan Witters, "U.S. Depression Rates Reach New Highs," Gallup, May 17, 2023, https://news.gallup.com/poll/505745/depression-rates-reach-new-highs.aspx.

27. Jon Haidt, "Social Media Is a Major Cause of the Mental Illness Epidemic in Teen Girls. Here's the Evidence," After Babel, February 22, 2023, https://jonathanhaidt.substack.com/p/social-media-mental-illness-epidemic.

28. Robert D. Putnam, *Bowling Alone: Revised and Updated: The Collapse and Revival of American Community*. New York: Simon & Shuster, 2020, 421.

29. Sherry Turkle, *Alone Together: Why We Expect More from Technology and Less from Each Other* (New York: Basic Books, 2011), 153.

30. Turkle, footnote 2, 329.

30. Putnam, *Bowling Alone*, 431.

32. Mary Shelley, *Frankenstein* (New York: Barnes & Noble Classics, 2003), 143.

33. "Home Page," American Atheists, accessed June 1, 2023, www.atheists.org/.

Conclusion

1. Peter Kreeft, *Wisdom of the Heart: The Good, the True, and the Beautiful at the Center of Us All* (Gastonia, NC: TAN Books, 2020), 238.

2. Leo Tolstoy, *Anna Karenina*, trans. Constance Garnett (New York: Modern Library, 2000), 921.

3. Tolstoy, 923.